Introduction to Database Management

Project Manual

Frank Miller

BICENTENNIAL
1807
WILEY
2007
BICENTENNIAL

ACQUISITIONS EDITOR	Lois Freier
MARKETING MANAGER	Jennifer Slomack
PRODUCTION MANAGER	Kelly Tavares

To order books or for customer service please, call 1-800-CALL WILEY (225-5945).

ISBN- 978-0-470-11410-0

Printed by R. R. Donnelley

10 9 8 7 6 5 4 3 2 1

PREFACE

Introduction to Database Management Project Manual is a learning tool for individuals who are new to database management, as well as those who seek to expand their skills in the field. It is an ideal companion to Gillenson et al.'s *Introduction to Database Management (Copyright 2008, John Wiley & Sons, 9-780-470-10186-5).*

Easy-to-read, practical, and up-to-date, this Project Manual includes activities that reinforce the fundamentals of database design and management concepts while helping students develop core competencies and real-world skills. The sheer variety and span of activities let students learn at their own pace.

Each chapter contains five to seven projects. Projects range from easy to more advanced, and many include multiple parts. Each project contains the following elements:
- **Overview:** Introduces the topic of the project, and reviews relevant concepts.
- **Outcomes:** Lists what students will know how to do after completing the project.
- **What You'll Need:** Lists specific requirements for the project
- **Completion Time:** Provides an estimated completion time as a guide. (Actual completion times may vary depending on experience levels.)
- **Precautions:** Notes on issues that should be taken into account prior to undertaking the project.
- **Projects:** A variety of project types are included. The majority of projects involve hands-on activities in which students are guided through the steps required to accomplish a task. Some projects involve case-based scenarios, while others assess student familiarity with basic concepts through matching and other paper-and-pen exercises. Many of the projects include multiple parts related to the project topic.
- **Assessment questions:** Embedded within each project, these questions help students assess their understanding as they go.
- **Graphic Elements:** Each project contains screenshots, conceptual graphics and/or tables that help inform and guide students as they proceed through the project.

After completing the activities in this Project Manual, users will be able to:
- Install SQL Server 2005
- Read and create an ERD
- Design and implement a database
- Use DDL and DML commands
- Use and monitor transactions
- Manage security principles, permissions, and backups
- Design data environments
- Use replication

CONTENTS

Important Note about Completing the Activities in this Manual:
For all activities that require documents and other content not included in this printed Project Manual, please visit the Book Companion Site indicated on the back of this manual. Once there, click on Student Companion Site at the upper right of the page, then Project Manual, then the chapter in which the activity appears.

1
INTRODUCING DATA AND DATA MANAGEMENT

PROJECTS

Project 1.1	Identifying Business Data
Overview	A key part of any database design is identifying business data. This can be a daunting task. Your first step is to identify the core business and, from this, primary tasks.
Outcomes	After completing this project, you will know how to: ▲ identify the core business ▲ identify primary tasks ▲ identify business documents
What you'll need	To complete this project, you will need: ▲ the worksheet below
Completion time	15 minutes
Precautions	None

You have descriptions of business activity for two businesses. Read each of the descriptions and then, in your own words, describe:

- the core business
- the steps in the example primary task
- potential data sources

■ Part A: Case #1

Regular customers prefer this business because the produce is farm fresh, delivered by the farmers each morning. Most items are sold by the pound. Customers make their own selections and bring them to the counter to be weighed. The total is calculated as cost per pound times weight plus sales tax. Each customer is given a cash register receipt. Volume customers get a detailed, handwritten invoice on request. All customers pay by cash or check.

1. What is the core business?

   _____

   _____

   _____

2. Describe the primary task steps related to the business activity in the minicase, as they apply to a standard customer.

    _____

    _____

    _____

3. What, if any, business documents are generated?

    _____

    _____

    _____

■ Part B: Case #2

Pickup and drop-off arrangements are generally made by the customer, by phone or over the Internet, or through a travel agency. If arrangements are made over the Internet, the customer receives a confirmation e-mail. Otherwise, the confirmation number is given over the phone. The driver picks up the customer and any additional passengers based on the arrangements made and delivers them to the drop-off point. Depending on the advance arrangements, the driver may be required to make multiple stops and wait at each stop. The trip invoice is printed in advance, and the driver is not authorized to make any changes to the route or stops. Payment by cash or credit card is required, with prepayment preferred. The customer is given a copy of the trip invoice at the last stop.

1. What is the core business?

    _____

    _____

    _____

2. Describe the primary task steps related to the business activity.

    _____

    _____

    _____

3. What, if any, business documents are generated?

    _____

    _____

    _____

Project 1.2	Identifying Human Data Sources
Overview	Employee and manager interviews are common sources of data. They also help identify key business documents. However, you need to know both who and what to ask.
Outcomes	After completing this project, you will know how to: ▲ match questions to correct employee level
What you'll need	To complete this project, you will need: ▲ the worksheet below
Completion time	10 minutes
Precautions	None

You need to interview employees at a department store to get business information and identify business documents. For each type of information, mark the question as A for executive management, B for midlevel and front-line management, or C for employee. Pick the best choice for each question.

___ Long-term business goals

___ Procedure for looking up prices

___ Procedure for looking up the store's purchase cost for a merchandise option

___ Vendor list for restocking orders

___ Steps to complete a sale to a customer

___ Merger plans

___ How to post a return

___ Who gives final approval for vacations

___ Gross sales and profit for the most recent calendar year

___ Operating budget for the warehouse department

____Current inventory levels by department

____ How to log on at a computerized cash register

Project 1.3	Installing SQL Server 2005 Evaluation Edition
Overview	Microsoft SQL Server 2005 (the most current version available when this project manual was written) is a popular database management program. Several editions are available to meet the needs of various businesses and database applications. Evaluation Edition can be downloaded from Microsoft at no charge and lets you take SQL Server on a 180-day "test drive."
Outcomes	After completing this project, you will know how to: ▲ install SQL Server installation prerequisites ▲ install SQL Server 2005 Evaluation Edition

What you'll need	To complete this project, you will need:
	
	▲ SQL Server 2005 Evaluation Edition installation software
	▲ a computer running Windows XP Professional or Windows Server 2003. The computer must meet the following hardware minimums:
	
	    • 500 MHz Pentium III process (or better)
	    • 512 MB RAM (or more)
	    • 1 GB free hard disk space (or more)

Completion time	90 minutes
Precautions	Be sure to check with your system administrator before installing on a school networked client computer. You will need an administrator user name and password to complete the installation. Later exercises will require Internet access. If you see any prompts during installation that do not match the steps provided here, ask your instructor for assistance.

1. If necessary, start the computer and log on as an administrator.
2. Insert the **SQL Server 2005 Evaluation Edition** installation disk.
3. Let the disk autorun and choose **Server components, tools, Books Online, and samples** from Installation or navigate to **\Server** and run **Setup.exe**.
4. Check **I accept the licensing terms and conditions** and click **Next**.
5. In the **Installing Prerequisites** dialog box, click **Install**. The installation program will install all prerequisites.
6. After the prerequisites finish installing, click **Next**.

7. When the **Welcome** screen of the **SQL Server Installation Wizard** appears, click **Next** to start the installation.

8. Review the **System Configuration Check** dialog box and click **Next** to continue. Warnings on the system configuration check, like the one shown in Figure 1-1, will NOT prevent you from installing SQL Server on the computer.

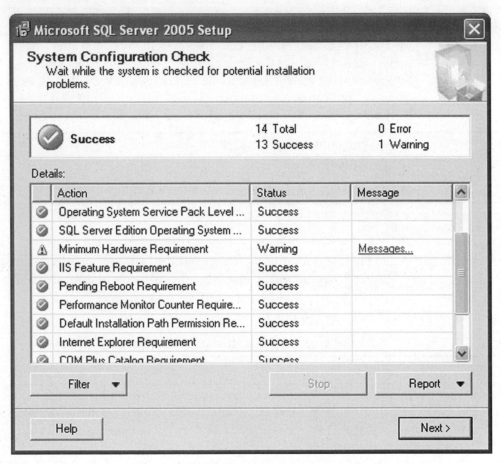

Figure 1-1: Configuration check warning

9. Verify or enter your name and any information in the **Company** field. Your instructor may provide you with a specific name to use in the this field. Click **Next** to continue.

10. In the **Components to Install** dialog box, check **SQL Server Database Services**, **Integration Services**, and **Workstation components, Books Online and development tools**. Your screen should look like the example in Figure 1-2.

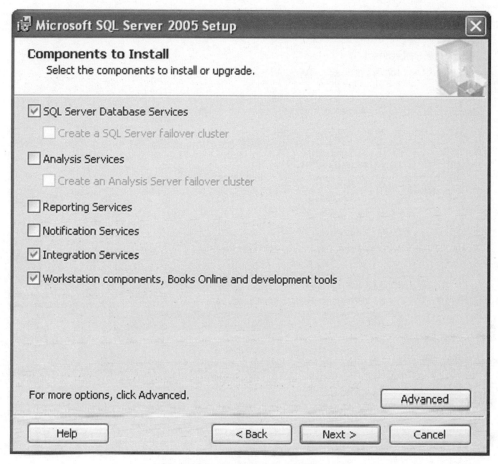

Figure 1-2: Installation selections

11. Click **Advanced**.

12. Expand **Documentation, Samples, and Sample Databases**.

13. The sample databases do not install by default. You will need the sample databases for later exercises. Click **Sample Databases** and choose **Entire feature will be installed on local hard drive**, as shown in Figure 1-3.

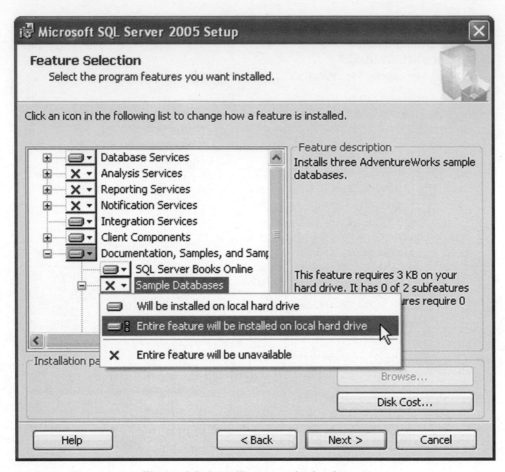

Figure 1-3: Installing sample databases

14. Click **Sample Code and Applications** and choose **Entire feature will be installed on local hard drive**. Your feature selections should look like Figure 1-4.

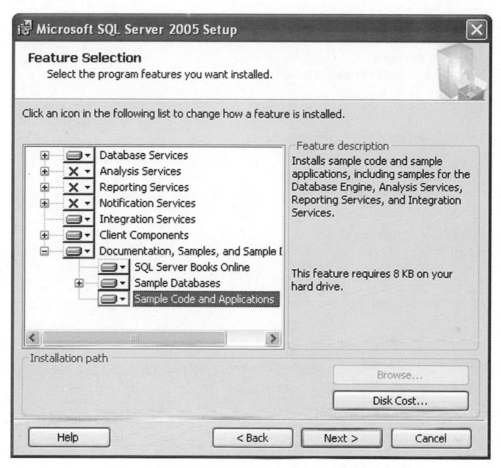

Figure 1-4: Completed advanced feature selections

15. Click **Next**.

16. Leave **Default instance** selected and click **Next**. The first instance, the first copy of SQL Server running on the computer, installs as the default instance. You can have other copies running as independent database servers under different names on the same computer.

17. In the **Service Account** dialog box, choose **Use the built-in system account**. You would typically not use this account in a secure production environment for security reasons.

18. Under **Start features at end of setup,** check **SQL Server Agent** and **SQL Browser**. Your selections should look like the example in Figure 1-5.

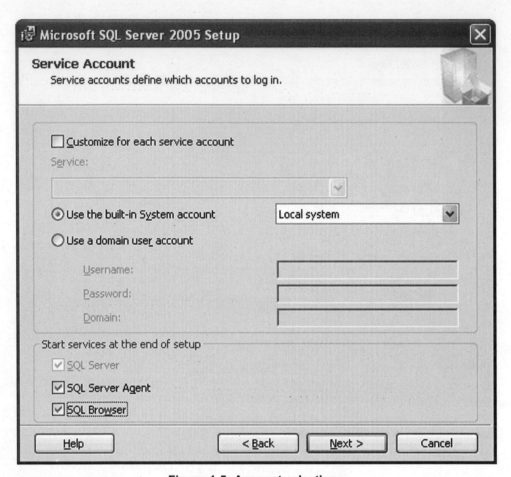

Figure 1-5: Account selections

19. Click **Next**.

20. When prompted for an authentication mode, select **Mixed Mode.** You must provide a password for the sa (system administrator) user. This user has unlimited access to the database server and all databases. Unless provided a different password by your instructor, enter **P@55word** as the password and then click **Next**.

21. Leave **Collation Settings** at default and click **Next**, as shown in Figure 1-6. Collation settings determine the character set used and the default sort order.

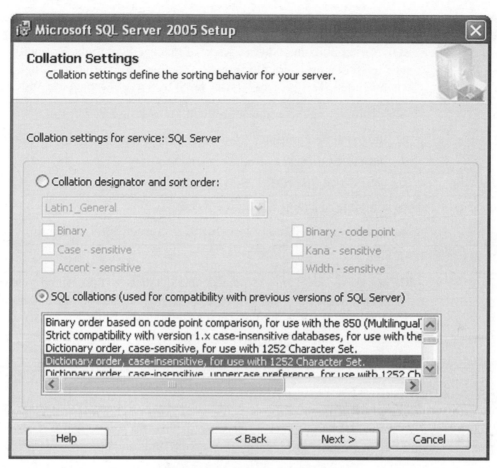

Figure 1-6: Collation settings

22. Leave the **Error and Usage Report Settings** at default and click **Next**.

23. Review the components on the **Ready to Install** dialog box list and click **Install**. This starts the installation. A dialog box informs you of installation progress.

24. When the installation is complete, click **Next**.

25. Click **Finish**. You have installed SQL Server 2005 Evaluation Edition.

Project 1.4	Learning About SQL Server Management Studio
Overview	SQL Server 2005 includes a variety of management tools. You will use selected tools throughout the course. You need to be able to launch the tools when needed. This project focuses on SQL Server Management Studio.
Outcomes	After completing this project, you will know how to: ▲ identify the computer (and SQL Server database server) name ▲ launch SQL Server Management Studio ▲ shut down and restart SQL Server
What you'll need	To complete this project, you will need: ▲ a computer running Microsoft SQL Server 2005 Evaluation Edition
Completion time	45 minutes
Precautions	Do not make any changes to the sample databases. If prompted to save changes when exiting any utility, choose No. The steps provided here assume you are running SQL Server 2005 on Windows XP Professional.

■ PART A: Identifying the server name

You installed a default instance of SQL Server. Because of this, the server name is also used as the database server name. You need to identify the server name.

1. Click **Start** and then open the **Control Panel**.
2. If the **Control Panel** is in **Category View**, click **Switch to Classic View**. The classic view is shown in Figure 1-7.

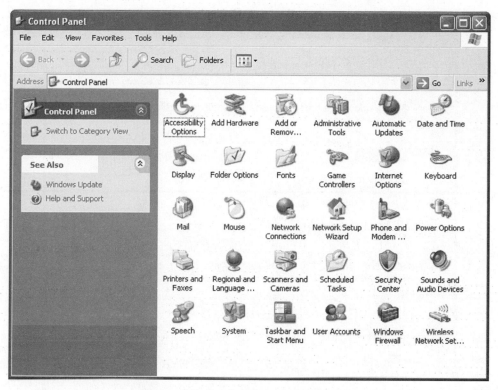

Figure 1-7: Control Panel classic view

3. Right-click **System** and choose **Open**.

4. Click the **Computer Name** tab and locate the **Full computer name** field. This field is shown in Figure 1-8.

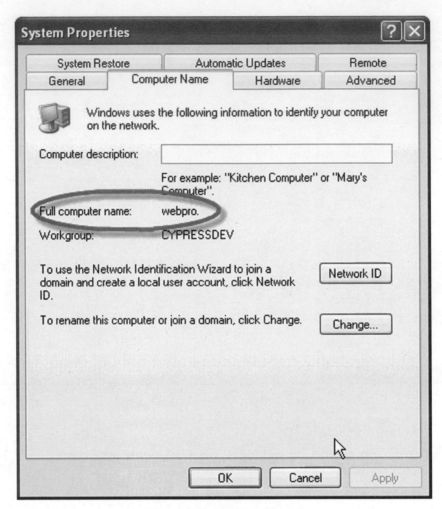

Figure 1-8: Computer name

5. Record the name:

_____

_____

6. Click **Cancel** to exit the **System** utility.
7. Close the **Control Panel**.

■ Part B: Becoming familiar with SQL Server Management Studio

SQL Server Management Studio is the utility that you will most often use when working with SQL Server during this course. It is also the primary management and administration tool in a production environment. You need to be familiar with a few basics. You should be logged in as an administrator user before starting this portion of the project.

1. Click **Start,** point to **All Programs**, select **Microsoft SQL Server 2005**, and then click **SQL Server Management Studio.**

2. When prompted to connect, verify that your computer name is in the **Server name** list box and that **Windows Authentication** is selected as the authentication type, as shown in Figure 1-9. Click **Connect**.

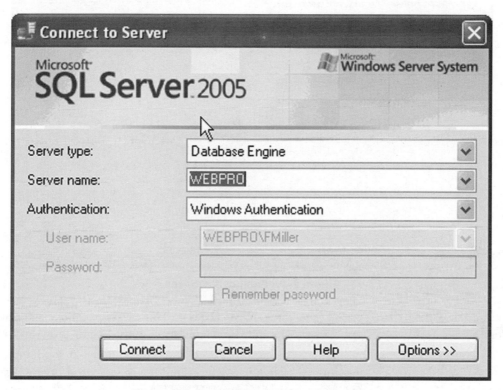

Figure 1-9: Sample Connection dialog box

3. The pane on the left is the **Object Explorer**. The folders you see are containers for databases, utilities, and server-level objects. Click the plus to the left of **Database** to expand that folder.

4. You should see databases named **AdventureWorks** and **AdventureWorksDW**, as shown in Figure 1-10. These are the sample user databases. You will be using these occasionally in class.

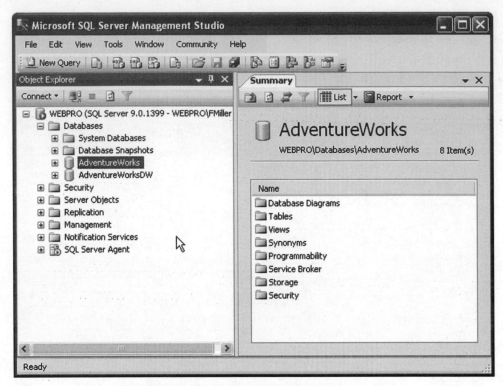

Figure 1-10: Sample databases

5. Right-click **AdventureWorks** and click **New Query**. This opens a query window. The query window is where you will most often be executing commands to view and manage database data.

6. In the toolbar above the query window, you should see a drop-down list with **AdventureWorks** selected as shown in Figure 1-11. This is your default database, also called the working database. Commands that run against a database or the data it contains will assume this database, unless a different database is specified.

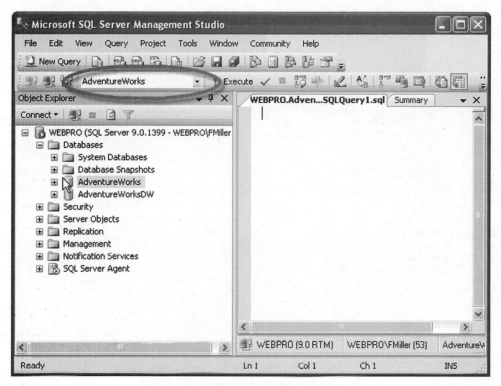

Figure 1-11: Default (working) database

7. Click the drop-down list. What other database names do you see listed?

_____

_____

   Most of these are known as system databases. They are a necessary part of SQL Server 2005. During this course, you won't be doing much with the system databases.

8. Choose **AdventureWorks** so it remains the default database.

9. Type the following in the query window:

```
SELECT * FROM Person.Contact
```

   Tip: The command is not case sensitive, so you don't have to worry about matching case.

10. Press **F5** to execute this command. This is the basic procedure for executing commands in a query window. You'll be shown additional details later in the course. This returns data to a pane identified as the **Results** page.

11. Next to the **Results** tab, you should see a tab for **Messages**. Click this tab to view any messages returned by the database server.

12. Click the **X** in the upper-right corner of the query window shown in Figure 1-12. This closes the query window.

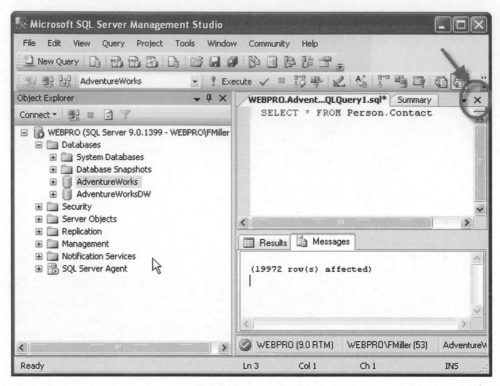

Figure 1-12: Close button

13. A dialog box prompts you to save changes. Click **No**.

14. Expand each of the remaining top-level folders so you can see what is contained in each.

▪ Part C: Shutting down and restarting SQL Server

You might occasionally find it necessary to shut down and restart SQL Server. One way to do this is through Management Studio.

1. In the **Object Explorer** pane, right-click your server name and choose **Stop**. Click **Yes** when prompted to verify your action.

2. When prompted to also stop **SQL Server Agent**, click **Yes**.

3. When the progress dialog box closes, you have shut down SQL Server.

4. To start SQL Server, right-click your server name and choose **Start**. Click **Yes** when prompted to verify your action.

5. When the progress dialog box closes, you have restarted SQL Server. Ask your instructor for assistance if an error dialog box appears. Exit Management Studio.

Project 1.5	Identifying Key Management Areas
Overview	One of the early tasks in design and development is identifying key management tasks. Management areas can be used to enforce a rough organization on identified tasks.
Outcomes	After completing this project, you will know how to: ▲ match management tasks to key management areas
What you'll need	To complete this project, you will need: ▲ the worksheet below
Completion time	10 minutes
Precautions	None

You need to match management tasks to task categories. Make the best selection for each task. Although task categories can be used more than once, you might not use some tasks. The task categories are:

A - Server Access Security

B - Physical Security

C - Data Organization

D - Data Access

E - Data Accuracy

____ Set limits on who can run commands to view table data

____ Assign logins and passwords

____ Identify important data

____ Decide how data will be represented in the database

____ Deploy the server in a locked room

____ Identify primary tasks performed by each user

____ Implement RAID storage

____ Reduce the server attack surface area

2
INTRODUCING DATABASES AND DATABASE MANAGEMENT SYSTEMS

PROJECTS

Project 2.1	Comparing Database Models
Overview	Database systems currently in use include a mix of the standard database models. Most new databases and applications are PC based, deployed on PC networks, and use a form of the relational model.
Outcomes	After completing this project, you will know how to: ▲ identify hierarchical database model features ▲ identify network database model features ▲ identify relational database model features ▲ identify object database model features
What you'll need	To complete this project, you will need: ▲ the worksheet below
Completion time	15 minutes
Precautions	None

You will be given a standard database model type and a series of statements. For each statement, circle T (for True) if the statement accurately describes the model and F (for False) if the statement does not accurately describe the model.

■ Part A: Hierarchical database model

T   F   Each child can have one and only one parent.

T   F   Each parent can have one and only one child.

T   F   This is the model most commonly used on PC-based database systems.

T   F   Relationships are established and maintained through the use of foreign keys.

T   F   A data structure can behave as both a parent and a child.

■ Part B: Network database model

T   F   This model derives its name because it can be deployed on a PC-based local area network only.

T   F   Relationships between members and owners are established through physical pointers.

T   F   An owner can have one and only one member.

T   F   A member can have one and only one owner.

T   F   This model forces record types into a hierarchical structure.

■ Part C: Relational database model

T   F   Relationships are maintained through physical pointers.

T   F   A single, definable type of item that you want to track in your database is known as an attribute.

T   F   This model can be used to represent data relationships that cannot be placed in a hierarchical model.

T   F   This model is commonly used with PC-based database systems.

T   F   This model is based on two-dimensional tables.

■ Part D: Object-oriented model

T   F   This is a legacy database model used on mainframe and minicomputers only.

T   F   This model can represent data not easily described through a hierarchical structure.

T   F   This model includes data types that can be used to represent multimedia-type data.

T   F   Features unique to this model include transaction processing and concurrency control.

T   F   This model includes support for abstract data typing.

Project 2.2	Identifying DBMS Architecture and Components
Overview	Part of understanding what you can and cannot do through your database design comes from having knowledge of database architecture. You also need to know the specific components supported by your DBMS.
Outcomes	After completing this project, you will know how to: ▲ identify DBMS architecture features ▲ identify the functionality provided by DBMS components
What you'll need	To complete this project, you will need: ▲ the worksheet below
Completion time	15 minutes
Precautions	None

Match each architectural component to the closest definition. Each component will be used only once.

____ Query processor

A. IT personnel who create and maintain databases, such as data modelers and programmers

____ Nonvolatile storage

B. Users who perform day-to-day functions that include retrieving and updating database data

____ Database engine

C. Component that lets you create screen layout and forms for data input and display

____ Forms generator

D. Automated and manual activities necessary for ongoing maintenance and update

____ Regular user

E. Industry-standard language for relational databases

____ Practitioner

F. Long-term secondary storage media such as a hard disk drive

____ Procedure

G. Checks a query for obvious syntax errors and determines resources available to run the query

____ Structured Query Language

H. Coordinates the tasks performed by all other DMBS components

Project 2.3	Reviewing Server Hardware Resources
Overview	Database server performance is directly impacted by server hardware resources. Before you can install your selected DBMS, the hardware must meet minimum installation requirements. Operational requirements depend on the amount of data you plan to store in the databases and how you plan to use the data.
Outcomes	After completing this project, you will know how to: ▲ identify processor resources ▲ identify main memory and how it is being used ▲ identify the number of physical and logical disk drives configured on the computer ▲ determine available disk space ▲ examine memory and processor configuration
What you'll need	To complete this project, you will need: ▲ a computer with SQL Server 2005 Evaluation Edition installed
Completion time	30 minutes
Precautions	When reviewing configuration settings, do not change any settings. If prompted to save changes when exiting any utility, choose not to save changes.

■ Part A: Determine hardware resources

1. Click **Start** and open the **Control Panel**. If the **Control Panel** is in **Category** view, switch to the **Classic** view.
2. Click **System** to open the **System Properties** dialog box. The processor and main memory are reported on the **General** tab, as shown in Figure 2-1.

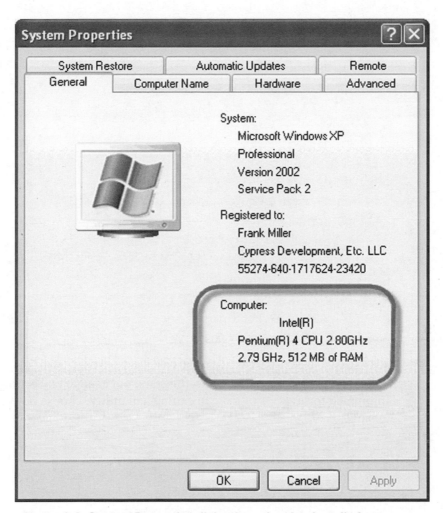

Figure 2-1: System Properties dialog box showing installed processor

3. What is the processor installed on your computer?

    _____

    _____

4. How much memory is installed on your computer?

    _____

    _____

5. Select the **Hardware** tab and click **Device Manager** (Figure 2-2). Expand **Disk drives** and **DVD/CD-ROM drives** (Figure 2-2).

Figure 2-2: Device Manager showing secondary storage

6. What hard disk drives are installed on your computer? What DVD or CD-ROM drives?

    _____

    _____

7. Open the **File** menu and click **Exit** to close Device Manager.
8. Click **Cancel** to close the **System Properties** dialog box.

■ Part B: View logical and physical hard disks

1. In the **Control Panel**, select **Administrative Tools** to open the **Administrative Tools** window.
2. In the **Administrative Tools** window, select **Computer Management** to open the **Computer Management** console.

3. Under **Storage**, select **Disk Management**, as shown in Figure 2-3.

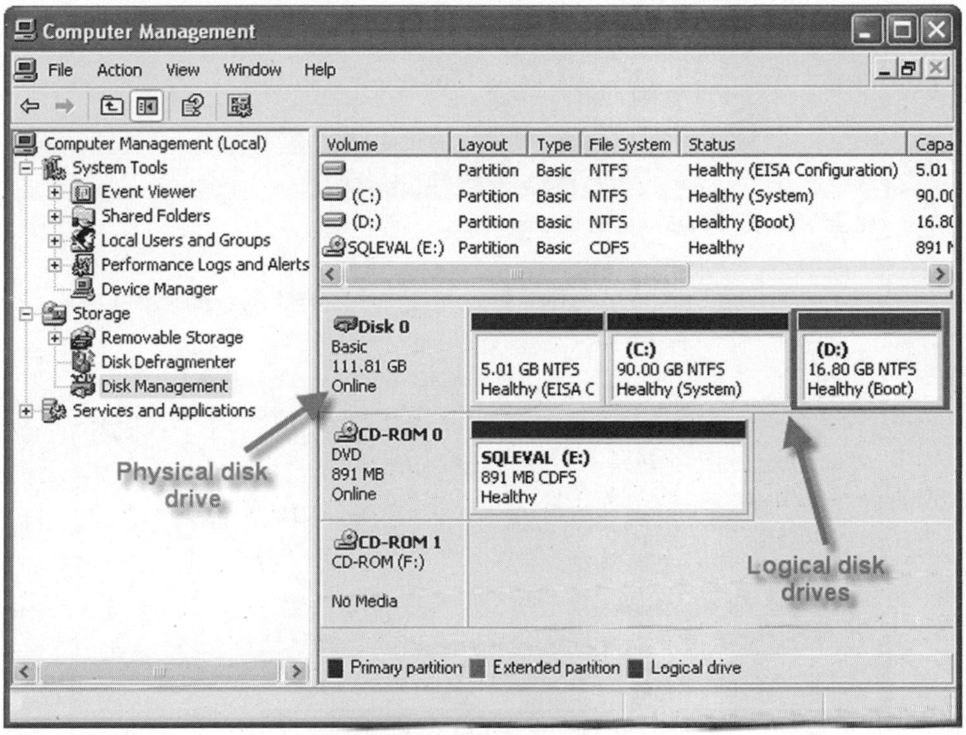

Figure 2-3: Disk Management

4. How do the hard disks and DVD/CD-ROM drives reported compare to those reported in the Device Manager? Record your answer below.

_____

_____

5. List the physical drives, logical drives, and sizes reported for drives in Table 2-1 below. If your computer has more than four logical drives, list the first four drives:

Table 2-1: Disk usage

Physical Drive Number	Logical Drive ID	Total Disk Space	Available Disk Space

6. Close the **Computer Management** console.
7. Close the **Administrative Tools** window.
8. Click **Start** and open the **My Computer** window.
9. Click **Folders** to view drives and folders, as shown in Figure 2-4.

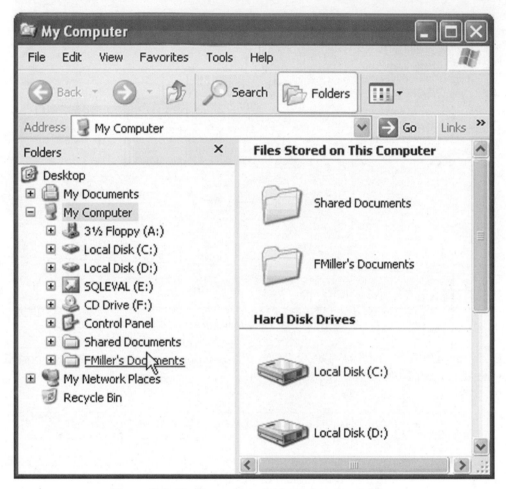

Figure 2-4: My Computer window showing folders

10. For each logical drive, right-click the drive and select **Properties** to open the **Properties** dialog box for the drive. Add the available disk space, indicated in Figure 2-5, to Table 2-1, and then click **Cancel** to close the **Properties** dialog box.

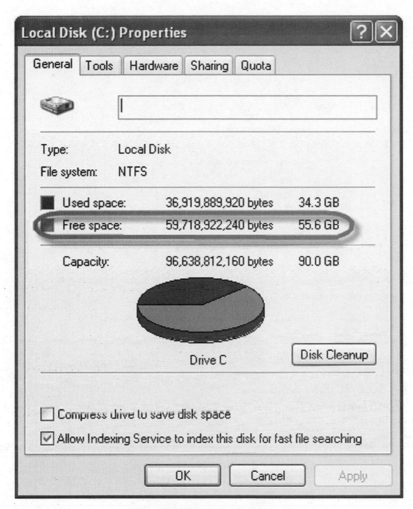

Figure 2-5: Available space

11. Close **My Computer**.

■ Part C: Examine memory and processor configuration

1. Click **Start**, point to **All Programs**, select **Microsoft SQL Server 2005**, and then click **SQL Server Management Studio**.
2. Click **Connect** to connect to your local server.
3. In the **Object Explorer** pane, right-click the server and select **Properties**.
4. In the left pane, choose **Memory** as shown in Figure 2-6. This shows you how this instance is configured to use memory.

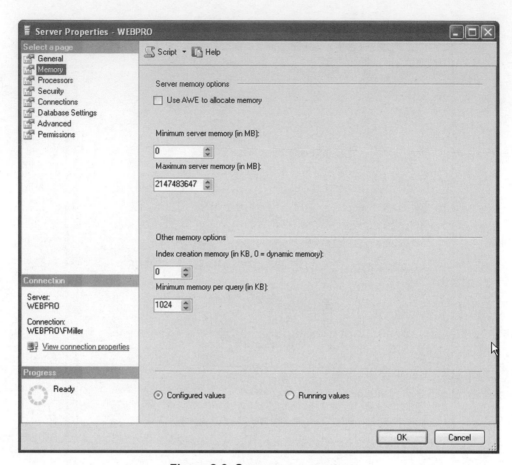

Figure 2-6: Server memory use

5. Click **Processors**, as shown in Figure 2-7. This shows you how this instance is configured to use available processors.

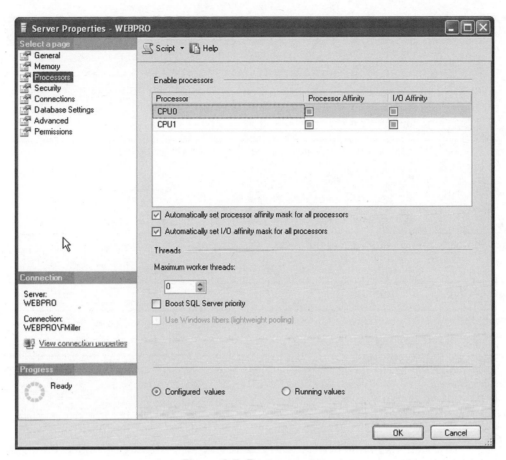

Figure 2-7: Processor use

Note: A computer running Windows XP that has a Pentium 4 HT processor will report two processors installed. Because of this, SQL Server will also report two microprocessors. This is because of how Windows XP detects and uses HT processors. The figures in this book are taken from a computer with a single Pentium 4 HT processor.

Project 2.4	Investigating SQL Server Databases
Overview	Databases are used for data storage. With SQL Server 2005, databases are also used to store metadata about the server instance, configuration settings, and user databases. It's important to understand the databases that are installed by default with SQL Server and how they are physically stored on the hard disk.
Outcomes	After completing this project, you will know how to: ▲ identify system databases ▲ identify user databases ▲ locate where database files are physically stored
What you'll need	To complete this project, you will need: ▲ a computer with SQL Server 2005 Evaluation Edition installed
Completion time	20 minutes
Precautions	If you have trouble locating the database files, ask your instructor for assistance.

■ PART A: View databases

1. If not already running, launch **SQL Server Management Studio** and connect to your local SQL Server instance.

2. Expand **Databases**, as shown in Figure 2-8.

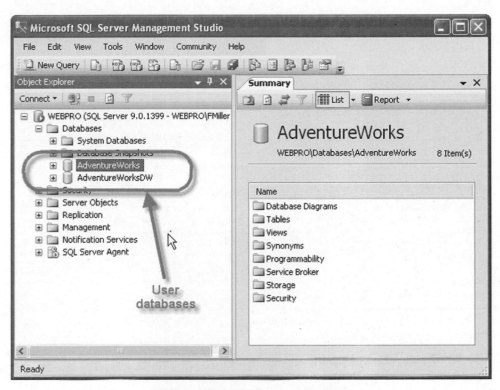

Figure 2-8: SQL Server databases

3. In addition to the **System Databases** and **Database Snapshots** folders, you should see one or more databases (indicated by the icon that looks like a canister). What databases are listed?

    _____

    _____

4. Expand **System Databases**. Record and explain what you see.

    _____

    _____

    _____

■ Part B: Viewing database information

1. Expand the **AdventureWorks** database (the first user database). The folders under the database are containers for database-specific objects. What folders do you see listed?

    _____

    _____

2. Right-click **AdventureWorks** and select **Properties**.

3. In the left-hand pane of the **Database Properties** dialog box, click **Files**, as shown in Figure 2-9.

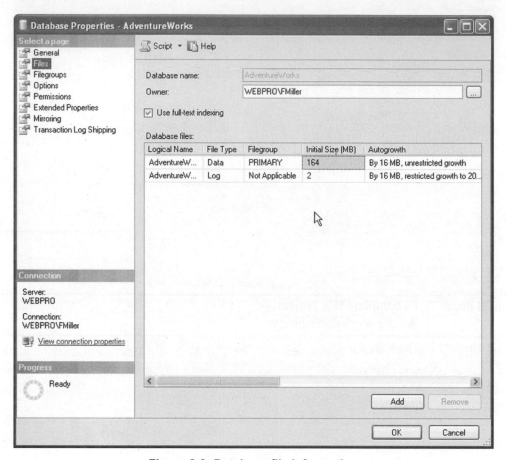

Figure 2-9: Database file information

4. List the logical file names below.

_____

_____

5. Exit the **Data Properties** dialog box and exit **Management Studio**.

6. Launch **My Computer** and navigate to the following location (assuming you installed SQL Server to the default location):

```
C:\Program Files\Microsoft SQL Server\MSSQL.1\MSSQL\Data
```

7. Locate the file names you recorded in step 4. These are the database (.mdf) and transaction log (.ldf) files for the AdventureWorks database. These files are the physical database.

8. For each of the files recorded in step 4, record the logical file name, physical file name (file name only, not complete path), and current file size in Table 2-2.

Table 2-2: File data

Logical File Name	Physical File Name	File Size

9. Exit **My Computer**.

Project 2.5	Identifying Application Requirements
Overview	Part of the database application design process is determining the components necessary to support a database application. These can include hardware resources, DBMS architectural components, and other components.
Outcomes	After completing this project, you will know how to: ▲ determine the components necessary to support an application ▲ identify whether necessary components are available
What you'll need	To complete this project, you will need: ▲ the worksheet below
Completion time	15 minutes
Precautions	None

Review the application description provided in each minicase. Answer the questions about hardware resources requirements.

■ Part A: Case #1

You are designing a database application. You plan to use SQL Server 2005 as the backend database. Server and client applications will be written using .NET Framework programming languages. The user interface and all reporting functions will be created as part of the client application.

The application will need to process several thousand transactions each day. Optimized performance during data retrieval and data update is critical to the application. A significant part of the data retrieval requirement includes several static look-up tables shared by different application components. The database must be backed up nightly to a file server located on the same network. You must ensure that these backups run at the same time every night.

1. Circle the components that would be most critical this application:

   Data engine
   Report writer
   Forms generator
   Query processor

2. What should you expect most of the available memory buffers to contain during normal processing?

   _____

   _____

   _____

   _____

3. Is processor speed important to this application? Why?

   _____

   _____

   _____

   _____

4. What kind of procedure would you use to ensure that backups run as needed? Record your answer below.

   _____

   _____

   _____

   _____

■ Part B: Case #2

You installed a database management system on a computer that meets the minimum installation requirements. The primary application involves data collection, retrieving data from automated sensors, and writing to the database tables. Based on the sensor sample rates, the application should never need to process more than one update at a time. The database is projected to eventually need to hold several million table rows. The data is critical, so the possibility of data loss must be minimized and the possibility of recovery after a failure must be maximized. Hardware and software costs on the collection database server must be kept to a minimum, investing in only those components key to meeting critical requirements.

Periodically, a separate application will retrieve all data from the collection database and copy the data to a separate online application processing (OLAP) decision support database for analysis and reporting. OLAP databases are used for this purpose and optimized for decision support data operation requirements. Data transfer will occur during scheduled maintenance periods when the sensors are taken offline so the activity does not interfere with data collection. Any existing data on the OLAP database will be overwritten by the process. The hardware platform for the OLAP database will not be purchased until after you can estimate its hardware resource requirements.

1. Which of the following would be key requirements in your collection database application design for normal operations?

    Read performance
    Write performance
    User interface
    Fault tolerant storage
    Report generation

2. Which of the following would be key requirements in your OLAP database application design for normal operations?

    Read performance
    Write performance
    User interface
    Fault tolerant storage
    Report generation

3. Of processor, memory, and hard disk, which current hardware resource is LEAST likely to meet the long-term requirements for collection database? Explain your reasoning.

    _____

    _____

    _____

    _____

4. Will the OLAP database meet your recovery requirements for the collection database? Why or why not? If not, describe (in general terms) how these requirements could be met.

    _____

    _____

    _____

    _____

3

DATA MODELING

PROJECTS

Project 3.1	Understanding Data Modeling Concepts
Overview	Before implementing a database as part of an application solution, you need to develop a database model. This is a logical representation of the physical database you plan to create. The better the model, the better your database and any applications based on that database.
Outcomes	After completing this project, you will know how to: ▲ identify key terms related to data modeling ▲ identify key terms related to relational database concepts
What you'll need	To complete this project, you will need: ▲ the worksheet below
Completion time	20 minutes
Precautions	None

The worksheet below includes a list of data modeling and relational database terms on the left and descriptions on the right. Match each term with the letter of its best description. You will use all descriptions. Each description can be used only once.

____ Entity

____ Attribute

____ Table

____ Index

____ View

____ Relationship

____ Logical design

A. Processes and procedures related to establishing and maintaining a relationship between table instances

B. Any item that you want to track as part of a database

C. Design process that includes identifying and implementing the physical database and database objects

D. An association defined and established between data entities

E. Information describing a data entity

F. Value setting the minimum number of entities that can be involved in a particular relationship

G. Value setting the maximum number of entities that can be involved in a particular relationship

____ Physical design

H. Data that are part of a many-to-many relationship and associated with a specific, unique instance of related entities

____ Primary key

I. Fundamental database object in the relational database model where entities are described as rows and columns

____ Cardinality

J. Relational database object that provides custom data retrieval

____ Modality

K. Entity designed to associate key values from two entities between which a many-to-many relationship is defined

____ Associative entity

L. Database object used to enforce uniqueness in a table

____ Intersection data

M. Design process that includes identifying entities and describing the data model

____ Referential integrity

N. Database object used to sort and organize data

Project 3.2	Recognizing Entities, Attributes, and Identifiers
Overview	An early part of the relational database design process is identifying entities. For each entity, you must identify its attributes. From this list of attributes, you will choose a unique attribute or set of attributes as the entity's identifier.
Outcomes	After completing this project, you will know how to: ▲ identify entities ▲ identify attributes ▲ select identifiers
What you'll need	To complete this project, you will need: ▲ the worksheet below
Completion time	30 minutes
Precautions	None

You will begin creating a relational database design based on each of the minicase studies provided below. Identify the entities described, and for each entity, identify the attributes included in the description and select an appropriate identifier

■ Part A: Case #1

You are designing a database application for an online grocer. Customers place orders over the Internet, and the orders are delivered to the customers' homes. Customers must live within 50 miles of a delivery warehouse. The company has 12 delivery warehouses in California.

Each employee has an employee ID. You also need to track the employee name and address, manager, and warehouse location at which the employee works. Each warehouse is identified for tracking purposes by a four-digit code. The application will use a mapping program to automatically qualify customers and assign the nearest warehouse for customer deliveries. A customer is assigned an ID when first registering at the company Web site. The customer must provide a contact name and phone number, address, and billing information.

Restocking orders are placed daily. Each vendor sells a wide range of items, and each inventory item can usually be ordered from at least two different vendors.

1. List the entities described in the case, including attributes and the best identifier.

_____

_____

_____

■ Part B: Case #2

You are designing a database for a service support company. Employees are tracked by social security number. You must also keep the employee name, address, phone number, department, and manager on file. Because married employees cannot both work in the same department per company policy, you must also track spouses for married employees.

The company provides business services for other companies. Along with a customer ID, you need to track the services provided. Detailed service records are kept that include coded values for the service provided, the rate, and the time to the nearest quarter hour.

Internally, the company tracks who provides what service for which customer, including the date and time the service was provided. This gives the company a reference in case of customer complaints.

Customers have up to 90 days to pay for services rendered. Billing records are tracked as under 30, 31 to 60, 61 to 90, and over 90. Customers with outstanding balances over 90 days old are placed on credit hold and cannot request additional services until payment is made.

1. List the entities described in the case, including attributes and the best identifier.

_____

_____

_____

_____

Project 3.3	Recognizing Relationships and Business Rules
Overview	Relationships are a defining part of relational database design. Relationships include one-to-one, one-to-many, and many-to-many relationships. Business rules place special restrictions on data.
Outcomes	After completing this project, you will know how to: ▲ identify unary and binary relationships ▲ identify one-to-one, one-to-many, and many-to-many relationships ▲ describe the appropriate use of intersection data
What you'll need	To complete this project, you will need: ▲ the worksheet below
Completion time	20 minutes
Precautions	None

Identify the relationships described in each minicase study as one-to-one, one-to-many, or many-to-many. Where appropriate, identify instances of intersection data.

■ Part A: Case #1

You are designing a database application for an online grocer. Customers place orders over the Internet and the orders are delivered to the customers' homes. Customers must live within 50 miles of a delivery warehouse. The company has 12 delivery warehouses in California.

Each employee has an employee ID. You also need to track the employee name and address, manager, and warehouse location at which the employee works. Each warehouse is identified for tracking purposes by a four-digit code. The application will use a mapping program to automatically qualify customers and assign the nearest warehouse for customer deliveries. A customer is assigned an ID when first registering at the company Web site. The customer must provide a contact name and phone number, address, and billing information.

Restocking orders are placed daily. Each vendor sells a wide range of items, and each inventory item can usually be order from at least two different vendors.

1. What unary relationships, if any, are described?

   _____

   _____

   _____

   _____

2. What one-to-one relationships are described?

   _____

   _____

   _____

   _____

3. What one-to-many relationships are described?

   _____

   _____

   _____

   _____

4. What many-to-many relationships are described?

   _____

   _____

   _____

   _____

5. What business rule is needed in relation to customers?

   _____

   _____

   _____

   _____

■ Part B: Case #2

You are designing a database for a service support company. Employees are tracked by social security number. You must also keep the employee name, address, phone number, department, and manager on file. Because married employees cannot both work in the same department per company policy, you must also track spouses for married employees.

The company provides business services for other companies. Along with a customer ID, you need to track the services provided. Detailed service records are kept that include coded values for the service provided, the rate, and the time to the nearest quarter hour.

Internally, the company tracks who provides what service for which customer, including the date and time the service was provided. This gives the company a reference in case of customer complaints.

Customers have up to 90 days to pay for services rendered. Billing records are tracked as under 30, 31 to 60, 61 to 90, and over 90. Customers with outstanding balances over 90 days old are placed on credit hold and cannot request additional services until payment is made.

1. What unary relationships are described? What kinds of relationships are they?

    _____

    _____

    _____

    _____

2. What relationships would you need to create for each service record?

    _____

    _____

    _____

    _____

3. What business rule is needed in relation to customers?

    _____

    _____

    _____

    _____

4. What business rule is needed in relation to employees?

_____

_____

_____

_____

Project 3.4	Reading an ERD
Overview	An ERD is a logical representation of a physical database design. To create a physical database, you must be able to accurately read and describe an ERD.
Outcomes	After completing this project, you will know how to: ▲ identify entities represented in an ERD ▲ identify relationships represented in an ERD
What you'll need	To complete this project, you will need: ▲ the worksheet below
Completion time	20 minutes
Precautions	None

Answer the questions below about the ERD diagram in Figure 3-1.

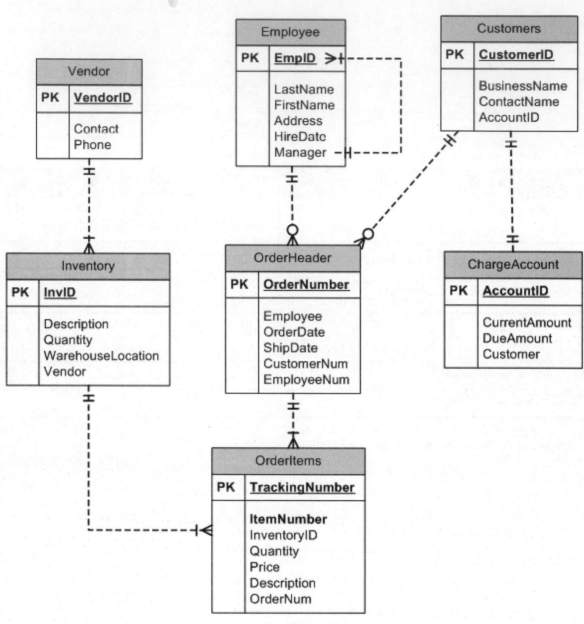

Figure 3-1: ERD diagram

1. What entities are shown in the model? Include the identifier for each entity.

    _____

    _____

    _____

    _____

2. Describe any one-to-one relationships shown in the model. Include relationship type.

_____

_____

_____

_____

3. Describe any one-to-many relationship shown in the model. Include relationship type.

_____

_____

_____

_____

4. Of the one-to-many relationships, which are one-to-zero-or-more relationships?

_____

_____

_____

_____

Project 3.5	Creating an ERD
Overview	During relational database design, you will create an ERD to represent the physical database. You need to be able to create an ERD based on a description of the business and the business data that you collect.
Outcomes	After completing this project, you will know how to: ▲ show entities in an ERD ▲ list attributes in an ERD ▲ draw simple relationships in an ERD
What you'll need	To complete this project, you will need: ▲ the business description provided below
Completion time	45 minutes
Precautions	None

Create an ERD to present the business model described. Use simple arrows to identify relationships between entities, as shown in Figure 3-2.

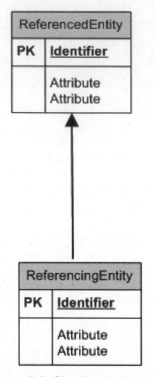

Figure 3-2: Simple relationship

You are designing an application for a professional equipment rental company. Each employee is assigned a unique employee ID. The company needs to track the employee last and first name, address, hire date, and manager. Managers are also employees.

Employees who work directly with customers are assigned responsibility for one or more customer accounts. Customer accounts include contact information, the customer address, and phone number.

For equipment with a serial number, that number is used for tracking purposes. Otherwise, a number is assigned internally as an item ID. The company needs to track the original vendor SKU (product number), purchase date, and current rental rate.

Employees are responsible for writing rental contacts for the customers. A customer can have one or more contracts on file. Each contract has a contract number and can include one or more rental items. The contract must identify the customer, items, rental date, and projected return date. Items are identified by an item number on the contract and by the item ID. If not returned by the return date, the employee responsible for that account is required to follow up with the customer. The application will generate daily reminder lists.

1.   What are the entities needed for the data model?

   _____

   _____

   _____

   _____

2.   What are the entity relationships and types?

   _____

   _____

   _____

   _____

3.   Sketch the data model.

Project 3.6	Viewing Basic Database Objects
Overview	Basic database objects include tables, views, and indexes. Tables are two-dimensional objects based on entities. Views provide specialized ways to view the table data, such as limiting columns or combining columns for different tables. Indexes sort and organize data.
Outcomes	After completing this project, you will know how to: ▲ identify how SQL Server organizes database objects ▲ investigate sample tables ▲ investigate sample views ▲ view the statement used to define a sample view ▲ investigate sample indexes ▲ create a database diagram based on selected tables
What you'll need	To complete this project, you will need: ▲ a computer with SQL Server 2005 Evaluation Edition installed ▲ the AdventureWorks database installed
Completion time	30 minutes
Precautions	You must be logged in as an administrator during this project. Do not make any changes to the computer or database server configuration while logged on as an administrator. Do not modify or delete any database objects.

■ Part A: Open the sample database

1. Click **Start**, point to **All Programs**, select **Microsoft SQL Server 2005**, and then click **SQL Server Management Studio**.
2. Click **Connect** to connect to your local server instance.
3. If not already expanded, expand your server instance in **Object Explorer**.
4. Expand **Databases**, then expand **AdventureWorks**.
5. In the **Object Explorer**, select **AdventureWorks** as shown in Figure 3-3.

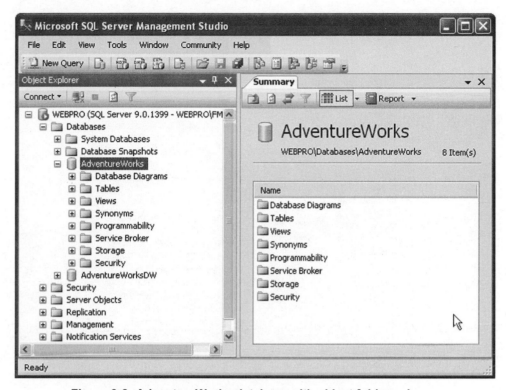

Figure 3-3: AdventureWorks database with object folders shown

■ Part B: Investigate tables

1. Expand **Tables**. Review the list of database tables. The tables contained in the **System Tables** folder are created and maintained by the database engine. These tables contain metadata for the database. Tables are identified by a two-part name. The first part is the schema, sometimes referred to as the relational schema. The relational schema is a way of organizing tables and managing security in a SQL Server 2005 database.

2. Locate and expand the **HumanResources.Employee** table.

3. Select **Columns** as shown in Figure 3-4.

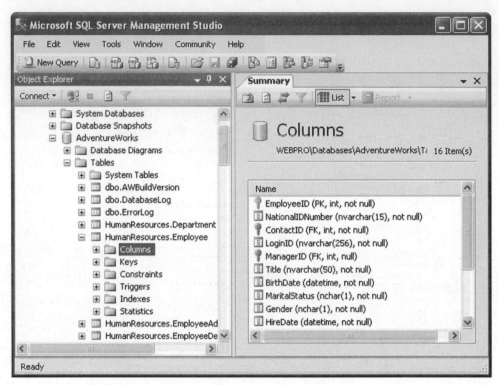

Figure 3-4: HumanResources.Employee table columns

4. What do these columns relate to in an ERD?

_____

_____

5. What is the table identifier?

_____

_____

6. The "FK" in parentheses identifies foreign keys. What foreign keys does the table contain?

_____

_____

■ **Part C: Investigate indexes**

1. Under **HumanResources.Employee**, expand and select indexes as shown in Figure 3-5.

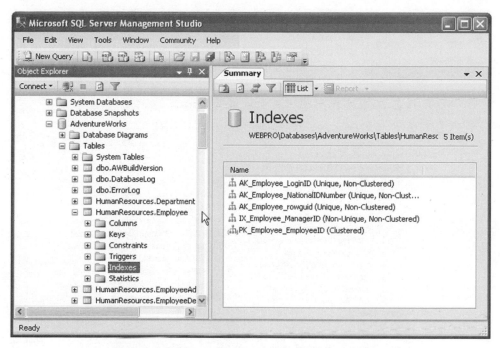

Figure 3-5: HumanResources.Employee Indexes

2. How does the index **PK_Employee_EmployeeID** differ from all other indexes listed here?

    _____

    _____

3. Which index does not require unique key values?

    _____

    _____

4. Right-click **PK_Employee_EmployeeID** and select **Properties**. What column or columns are used to define the index?

    _____

    _____

■ Part D: Investigating views

1. Collapse **Tables** (for easier viewing).
2. Expand **Views**.
3. Expand **HumanResources.vEmployeeDepartment**.
4. Expand **Columns** to see the columns included in the view, as shown in Figure 3-6.

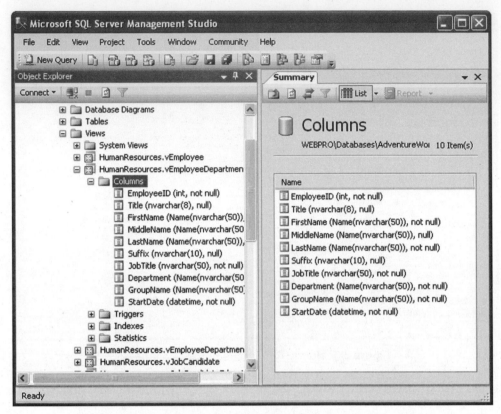

Figure 3-6: HumanResources.vEmployeeDepartment columns

5. Although it is somewhat beyond the current scope of this book, you can get an idea of what is involved in creating a view by choosing to modify it through Management Server. Right-click **HumanResources.vEmployeeDepartment** and choose **Modify** as shown in Figure 3-7.

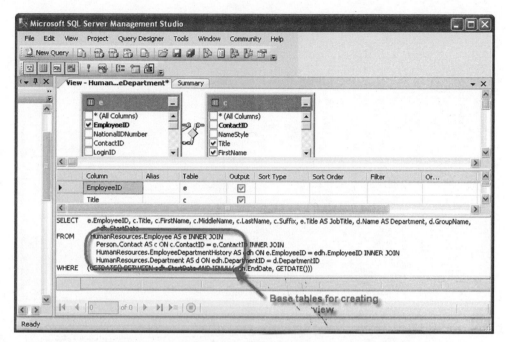

Figure 3-7: Modify dialog for HumanResources.vEmployeeDepartment

The table names "e" and "c" are aliases for actual table names. For example, "e" is the alias for HumanResources.Employee. The actual table names are visible in the SELECT statement in the third pane from the top.

■ Part E: Use database diagrams to view relationships and other information about database tables

1. Let's look at the relationships between the tables referenced in the statement used to create **HumanResources.vEmployeeDepartment**.

2. Maximize **Management Studio**.

3. Under **AdventureWorks**, right-click **Database Diagrams** and choose **New Database Diagram**.

4. For each of the following tables, select the table in the **Add Table** dialog box and then click **Add**:

   • Contact (Person)

   • Department (HumanResources)

   • Employee (HumanResources)

   • EmployeeDepartmentHistory (HumanResources**)**

5. Click **Close**. Your database diagram should look similar to the one shown in Figure 3-8.

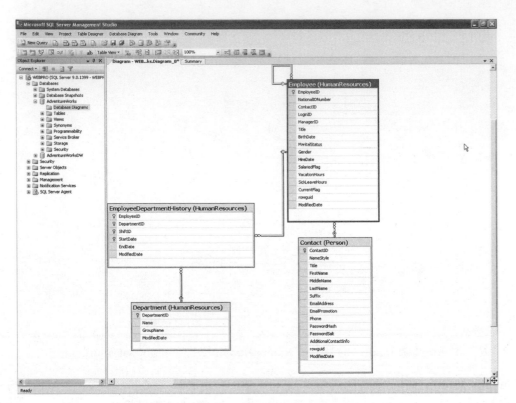

Figure 3-8: Sample database diagram

6. The database diagramming feature provides one option for documenting your database and comparing the final database to the original ERD. You can include any or all tables in the diagram. However, the more tables you add, the more complicated (and potentially hard to read) the diagram. For example, the diagram in Figure 3-9 includes all tables from the AdventureWorks database.

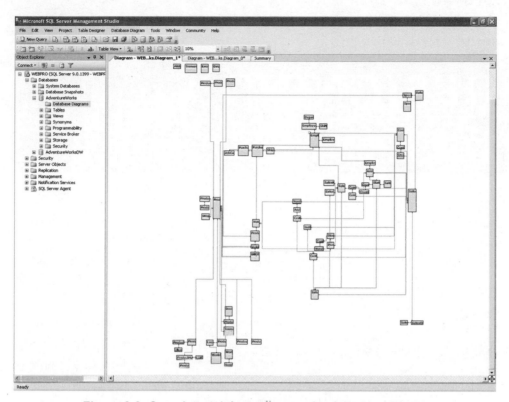

Figure 3-9. Complete database diagram for AdventureWorks

7. Open the **File** menu and click **Exit** to exit **Management Studio**. When prompted to save changes, click **No**.

4

DESIGNING A DATABASE

Project 4.1	Understanding Key Concepts
Overview	When creating your database design and making the move from entities to tables, it is important that you understand key terms and design concepts. A database is no better than its design, and a design is often no better than the designer's understanding of the fundamentals.
Outcomes	After completing this project, you will know how to: ▲ identify key terms and concepts related to converting entities to tables ▲ identify concepts related to data normalization
What you'll need	To complete this project, you will need: ▲ the worksheet below
Completion time	20 minutes
Precautions	None

The worksheet includes a list of data modeling and relational database terms on the left and descriptions on the right. Match each term with the description that it most closely matches. You will use all descriptions. Each description can be used only once.

____ Unary relationship

____ Binary relationship

____ Third normal form

____ Second normal form

____ First normal form

____ Nonloss decomposition

____ Entity

A. Normalization requirement that prohibits transitive dependencies

B. A condition in which one nonkey attribute is functionally dependent on another nonkey attribute

C. In data normalization, referring to each attribute having a single value

D. Basic data storage object in a relational database

E. Normalization requirement that every nonkey attribute must be fully functionally dependent on the entire primary key

F. A means of expressing that the value of one particular attribute is associated with a single, specific value of another attribute

G. A relationship defined between two entities

___	Table	H. A dependency where data is dependent on part, but not all, of a primary key
___	Relationship	I. Referring to less commonly used normalization forms
___	Exception condition	J. An association between two entities or between an entity and itself
___	Functional dependency	K. A relationship defined between an entity and itself
	Transitive dependency	L. Normalization process in which neither data nor relationships are lost
___	Partial functional dependency	M. A single "thing" tracked by a database and typically represented in a database as a table
___	Atomic	N. Normalization requirement that each attribute value, and therefore each table column, is atomic

Project 4.2	Converting Relationships
Overview	A critical step in the database design process is converting the entities identified in the logical design into database tables. This includes converting the relationships between entities.
Outcomes	After completing this project, you will know how to: ▲ convert unary relationships ▲ convert binary relationships ▲ recognize and convert one-to-one, one-to-many, and many-to-many relationships
What you'll need	To complete this project, you will need: ▲ the worksheet below
Completion time	45 minutes
Precautions	None

You will be presented with a description of a relationship followed by one or more entity diagrams. With some descriptions, you will also be provided with an empty entity form. Instructions are provided with each relationship.

■ Part A: Relationship #1

Not all employees are salespersons. Each salesperson is assigned direct responsibility for one or more customers. Each customer is assigned exactly one salesperson.

	Employee
PK	<u>EmployeeID</u>
	EmployeeName EmployeeAddress WorkExtension HomePhone

	Customer
PK	<u>CustomerID</u>
	CustomerName ContactName CustomerAddress PrimaryPhone

Figure 4-1: Entities for Relationship #1

1. What value should you use as a foreign key?

____

____

2. Where should the foreign key be placed?

____

____

3. To what attribute will the foreign key relate?

____

____

4. What attributes, if any, are necessary to complete the relationship?

____

____

■ Part B: Relationship #2

Each employee must be uniquely identified. Each employee will have a manager. A manager is responsible for one or more employees. The company owner manages him- or herself. The only reliably unique value is EmployeeID.

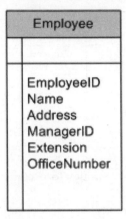

Figure 4-2: Entities for Relationship #2

1. What should you use as the primary key?

    _____

    _____

2. What type of relationship is defined by this description?

    _____

    _____

3. What should you use as the foreign key?

    _____

    _____

4. To what value would the foreign key relate?

    _____

    _____

5. What attributes, if any, are necessary to complete the relationship?

    _____

    _____

■ Part C: Relationship #3

Each customer is uniquely identified by a CustomerID. Each order is uniquely identified by an OrderNumber. Each order is made up of an OrderHeader and one or more OrderDetails. A customer can have zero or more orders on file at any time.

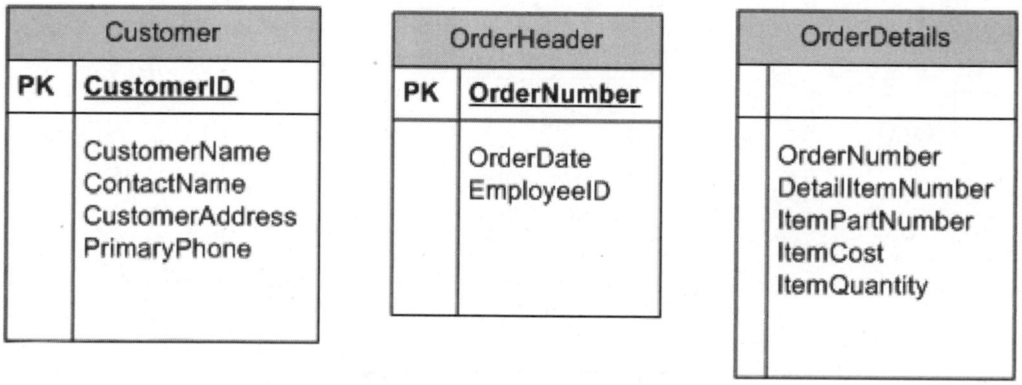

Customer	
PK	**CustomerID**
	CustomerName ContactName CustomerAddress PrimaryPhone

OrderHeader	
PK	**OrderNumber**
	OrderDate EmployeeID

OrderDetails	
	OrderNumber DetailItemNumber ItemPartNumber ItemCost ItemQuantity

Figure 4-3: Entities for Relationship #3

1. What should you use as the primary key in the OrderDetails table?

2. Describe the relationship between OrderHeader and Customer.

3. What should you use as a foreign key between OrderHeader and Customer? To what will it relate?

4. What should you choose as the foreign key in OrderDetails? To what should it relate?

5. The complete design should include two additional related tables. Describe them.

■ Part D: Relationship #4

Each vendor can supply hundreds of different products. Each product can be purchased from one or more vendors.

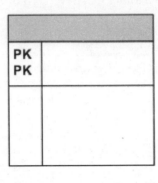

Figure 4-4: Entities for Relationship #4

1. What kind of relationship is described between Vendor and Product?

   _____

   _____

2. How will you maintain that relationship?

   _____

   _____

3. Describe the keys needed to enforce the relationship between Vendor and Product.

   _____

   _____

4. Update Figure 4-4 with additional attributes and entities as necessary.

Project 4.3	Reviewing a Normalized Database
Overview	Organizing entities and attributes into tables and columns is only part of an extended design and implementation process. After you identify your database tables, you have to take them through nonloss decomposition, the data normalization process.
	The rules for normalization, known as normal forms, are relatively simple and easy to understand. Their impact on database and table design can be significant, depending on how far you take the normalization process.
	Before starting on a new task, it helps if you understand the goal. You might find it helpful to see a database that has been normalized before attempting to do it yourself.
	The AdventureWorks database is an example of normalization taken to what some might consider an extreme. A potential problem in this, or in any database that you didn't design, is hunting out relationships between tables.
Outcomes	After completing this project, you will know how to:
	▲ view table properties
	▲ identify primary and foreign key assignments
	▲ locate related tables
What you'll need	To complete this project, you will need.
	▲ a computer with SQL Server 2005 Evaluation Edition installed
	▲ the AdventureWorks database installed
Completion time	30 minutes
Precautions	You should be logged on as an administrator during this project. Do not make any changes to the computer or database server configuration while logged on as an administrator. Do not modify or delete any database objects.

■ Part A: Open the sample database tables

1. Open the **Start** menu, point to **All Programs**, select **Microsoft SQL Server 2005**, and then click **SQL Server Management Studio**.
2. Click **Connect** to connect to your local server instance.
3. If not already expanded, expand your server instance in **Object Explorer**.
4. Expand **Databases**, and then expand **AdventureWorks**.
5. Expand and select **Tables**.

■ Part B: View sample tables

1. Expand **Sales.Customer** and select **Columns**. From this view, is there any way to determine which tables referenced or are referenced by **Sales.Customer**?

2. Expand **Sales.CustomerAddress** and select **Columns**. Notice that there are no columns for street, city, state, etc., but there is an **AddressID** foreign key column.

3. There is no **Sales.AddressID** table. Expand **Keys** and locate the foreign key **Customer_Address_AddressID**.

4. Double-click **Customer_Address_AddressID**.

5. In the **Foreign Key Relationships** dialog box, verify that **Customer_Address_AddressID** is selected in the **Tables and Columns Specification**.

6. When a browse button **(...)** displays, click it to open the **Tables and Columns** dialog box shown in Figure 4-5.

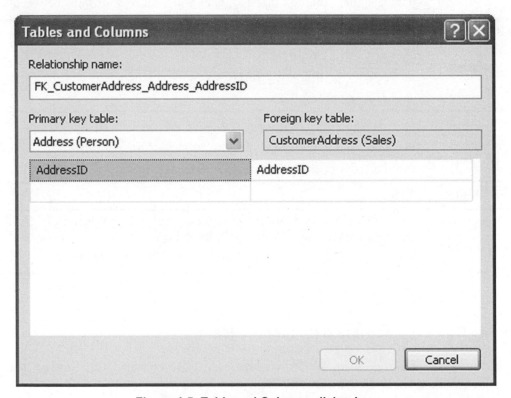

Figure 4-5: Table and Columns dialog box

7. What is the referenced table in this relationship?

_____

_____

■ Part C: View database diagrams

1. Right-click **Database Diagrams** and select **New Database Diagram.**
2. In the **Add Table** dialog box, select **Customer(Sales)** and click **Add**.
3. Click **Close**. Your database diagram should look like the example in Figure 4-6.

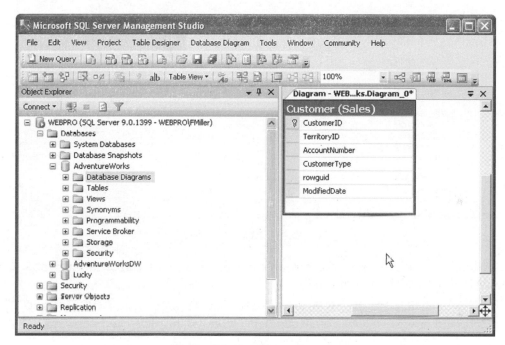

Figure 4-6: Database diagram

4. Right-click **Customer(Sales)** and select **Table View**, and then **Name Only**.
5. Right-click **Customer(Sales**) and select **Add Related Tables**.
6. While all of the tables are still selected, right-click any table and select **Table View**, and then **Name Only**. Your diagram should look like Figure 4-7, showing all of the tables directly relating to **Sales.Customer**.

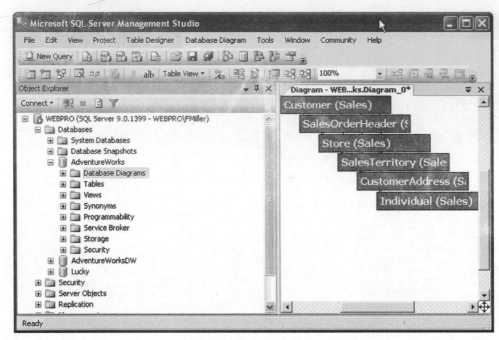

Figure 4-7: Related tables

7. Recall that there is at least one other table related to **Sales.CustomerAddress**. Click in the window so no tables are selected.

8. Right-click the table for **CustomerAddress(Sales)** and select **Add Related Tables**. What tables, if any, are added? What additional tables, if any, are highlighted and why?

   _____

   _____

9. Close the database diagram. Do not save changes if prompted.

Project 4.4	Recognizing Normalization Errors
Overview	To properly normalize a database, you must be able to recognize tables that do not adhere to one or more of the three basic normal forms: • First normal form - Each attribute value is atomic; that is, no attribute is multivalued. • Second normal form - Every nonkey attribute must be fully functionally dependent on the entire key. • Third normal form - Transitive dependencies are not allowed. The usual goal is to achieve 3NF, a database that is normalized to the third normal form.
Outcomes	After completing this project, you will know how to: ▲ identify multivalued columns ▲ identify partial functional dependencies ▲ identify transitive dependencies
What you'll need	To complete this project, you will need: ▲ the worksheet below
Completion time	30 minutes
Precautions	None

Below, you will be presented with a series of brief scenarios and tables. Each table contains a list of table columns and column descriptions. For each, identify the normal form(s) that each column violates (if any), and explain why. A column can violate multiple forms. Do not concern yourself with correcting the problems at this time.

1. Your company has offices in various geographic locations. Each employee is assigned to one specific geographic office. The only reliably unique value in the Employees table (see Table 4-1) is the EmployeeID column. Identify the normal form(s) that each column violates (if any), and explain why.

Table 4-1: Employees table

Column Name	Description	Form Violated	Justification
EmployeeID	Unique numeric value. Table primary key.		
Name	Employee's full name.		
OfficeID	Numeric value identifying the geographic office to which the employee is assigned.		
Extension	Employee's telephone extension.		
ManagerID	Foreign key relating to the employee's primary key and identifying the employee's manager.		
OfficeAddress	Full address for the office to which the employee is assigned.		
PayRate	Employee pay rate. Foreign key relating to another table.		

2. Call tracking documents customer service calls initiated by either the customer or the employee as a return call. The CallTracking table (see Table 4-2) has a three-part primary key based on the CustomerID, EmployeeID, and DateTime stamp of the call. Much of the information is entered automatically by a call tracking application. Identify the normal form(s) that each column violates (if any), and explain why.

Table 4-2: CallTracking table

Column Name	Description	Form Violated	Justification
CompanyID	Numeric value uniquely identifying the customer.		
EmployeeID	Numeric value uniquely identifying the employee.		
DateTime	Date/time stamp based on when the call started.		
ContactName	Full name of the person calling.		
CompanyName	Company name.		

Column Name	Description	Form Violated	Justification
Call duration	How long the call lasted in seconds.		
Followup	True/false field identifying whether this is a follow-up call.		
Call summary	Written summary of what was discussed during the call.		
Monitored	True/false field identifying whether the call was monitored by the employee's supervisor.		
SupervisorID	Employee's supervisor (manager).		
After hours	Whether the call occurred after normal business hours. Tracked for billing purposes.		
CustomerRate	Standard rate at which the customer is billed.		

3. Each inventory item in the Inventory table (see Table 4-3) is identified by an internally assigned inventory ID, which is used as the primary key. Each item will also have an SKU tracking number, which is also unique. Other fields are not necessarily unique. Identify the normal form(s) that each column violates (if any), and explain why.

Table 4-3: Inventory table

Column Name	Description	Form Violated	Justification
InventoryID	Numeric ID used as primary key.		
SKU	Identifying alphanumeric string.		
Description	Text description.		
Cost	Item cost.		
SellingPrice	Item selling price.		
QuantityOnHand	Quantity currently in the warehouse.		

Column Name	Description	Form Violated	Justification
Location	Where the item is located in the warehouse.		
Weight	Per unit weight.		
SellingVendor	Vendor from whom you purchase the item.		
VendorCustNum	Your customer number as assigned by the selling vendor.		

4. You work for a nonprofit organization that relies on donors for its survival. Each donor is assigned a unique donor ID in the Donors table (see Table 4-4). Identify the normal form(s) that each column violates (if any), and explain why.

Table 4-4: Donors table

Column Name	Description	Form Violated	Justification
DonorID	Numeric ID that uniquely describes the donor.		
DonorName	Donor's full name.		
DonorContact	Donor's contact information, including address and phone number.		
TotalDonation	Total amount donated by this donor.		
IsAnonymous	True/false field identifying whether the donor can be identified publicly.		
LastContact	Date of last contact with the donor.		
LastDonation	Date and amount of the donor's last donation.		
Referrals	Other persons referred by this donor.		

Project 4.5	Normalizing Data
Overview	You need to be able to identify tables that violate normal forms and redesign the tables so they adhere to normal forms.
Outcomes	After completing this project, you will know how to: ▲ recognize violations to normalization forms ▲ correct normalization errors
What you'll need	To complete this project, you will need: ▲ the following worksheet
Completion time	60 minutes
Precautions	None

The worksheet has a series of brief scenarios and table definitions. Each table definition has a list of table columns and column descriptions.

You are provided with blank table forms. Use these to redraw the tables as properly normalized (column names only). You are provided with four blank table forms for each exercise. You may not need all of the forms provided. Also, answer the follow-up questions, if any, provided with the scenario.

NOTE: You are creating partial table descriptions. The tables may require additional columns in the final design, but you do not have the information needed to define these columns. Limit your answers to the information you have been provided.

■ Part A: The Employees table

1. Refer to Table 4-1 in Project 4.4. Redraw Table 4-1 as properly normalized (column names only), using Figure 4-8.

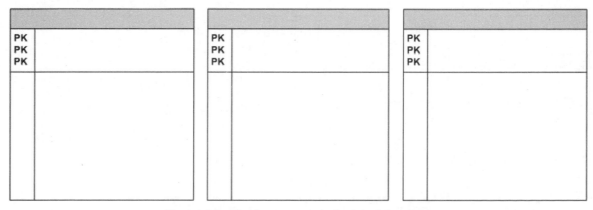

Figure 4-8: Employees scenario solution tables

2. What relationships were required by this solution?

_____

_____

3. How are any relationships defined (primary and foreign key requirements)?

_____

_____

■ Part B: The Donors table

1. Refer to Table 4-4 in Project 4.4. Design a solution in which TotalDonation is not needed as a table column.

2. Redraw Table 4-4 as properly normalized (column names only), using Figure 4-9.

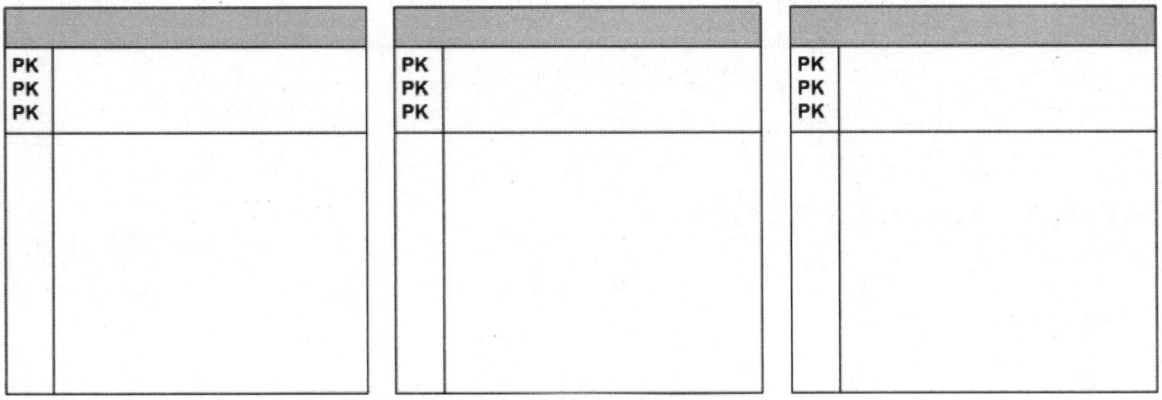

PK			PK			PK		
PK			PK			PK		
PK			PK			PK		

Figure 4-9: Donors scenario solution tables

3. What relationships were required by this solution?

_____

_____

4. How are they defined (primary and foreign key requirements)?

_____

_____

5. Why should LastDonation be tracked in a table separate from Donors?

_____

_____

■ **Part C: The CallTracking table**

1. Refer to Table 4-2 in Project 4.4 Redraw Table 4-2 as properly normalized (column names only), using Figure 4-10.

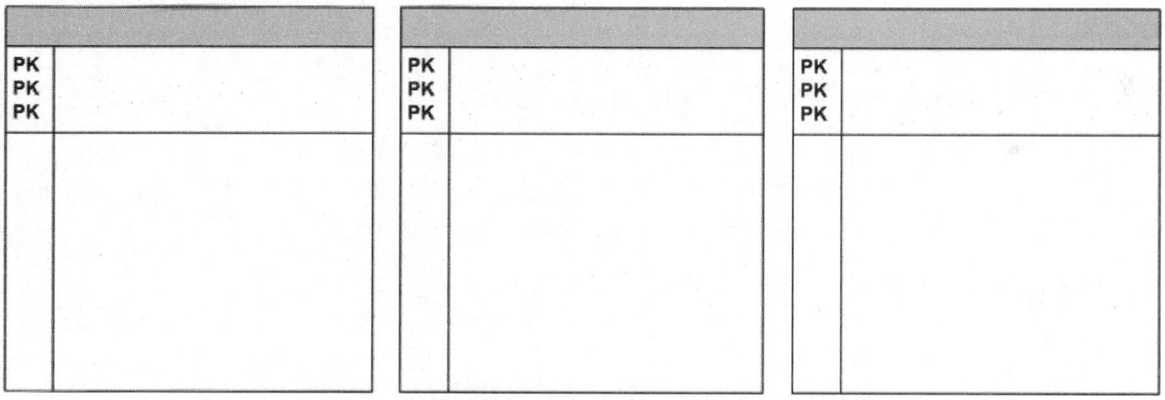

PK	
PK	
PK	

PK	
PK	
PK	

PK	
PK	
PK	

Figure 4-10: CallTracking scenario solution tables

2. What columns, if any, were you able to remove completely?

_____

_____

3. What relationships were required by this solution?

_____

_____

4. How are they defined (primary and foreign key requirements)?

_____

_____

5. How could you modify this solution to minimize the columns in the primary key? In general, would this affect the tables?

_____

_____

6. How could you link related calls to make it easier to locate earlier calls for reporting purposes?

_____

_____

5

IMPLEMENTING A DATABASE

PROJECTS

Project 5.1	Understanding Terms and Concepts
Overview	Implementing your database design includes selecting your DBMS and hardware platform, creating your databases, and creating your database objects. As with any other phase of the process, it is critical that you understand key terms and concepts.
Outcomes	After completing this project, you will know how to: ▲ identify key terms related to database implementation ▲ identify key concepts related to database implementation
What you'll need	To complete this project, you will need: ▲ the worksheet below
Completion time	20 minutes
Precautions	None

The worksheet includes a list of items on the left and descriptions on the right. Match each term with the description that it most closely matches. You will use all descriptions. Each description can be used only once.

____ Table

A. Database object used to sort and organize data

____ View

B. Database object that restricts a column to unique values

____ Index

C. Related to ensuring that the values entered in specified columns are legal

____ Trigger

D. Related to ensuring that relationships with other tables remain valid

____ Check constraint

E. In the context of tables, the processing of dividing data horizontally (by rows) or vertically (by columns)

____ Default constraint

F. Database object that lets you control the rows and columns a user can see and access

____ Unique constraint

G. Value representing "no value," either unknown, undefined, or no value applied

____ Entity integrity

H. Used to limit data values in a table column to a set range, part of a specified list, or to match a format pattern

____	Referential integrity	I. Process of upgrading database server hardware by improving the memory, processor, or other hardware resources
____	Domain integrity	J. Value entered when no value is provided for a column during data entry
____	Scale up	K. Data storage format used to specify storage characteristics for data columns and variables
____	Scale out	L. Basic data storage object structured as rows and columns
____	Partitioning	M. Related to ensuring that each row in a table is uniquely identified
____	Null	N. Process of partitioning data and a database application across multiple database servers
____	Data type	O. Executable database object that executes in response to a data modification or data definition event

Project 5.2	Identifying Solution Requirements
Overview	While moving a project from design to physical implementation, you must be able to identify solution requirements. These include hardware requirements, software requirements, and data design requirements.
Outcomes	After completing this project, you will know how to: ▲ identify conditions that affect hardware design ▲ identify conditions that affect software selection ▲ identify conditions that affect table design
What you'll need	To complete this project, you will need: ▲ the worksheet below
Completion time	45 minutes
Precautions	None

■ Part A: Case #1

You are designing a database application that will collect real-time information about manufacturing activity and factory conditions. The solution will be based on two databases, a production database that collects the data and a decision support database that processes the data for several reporting requirements. The production database will collect a week's worth of data. At the end of each week, the data is backed up for offsite archive, transferred to the decision support database, and deleted from the production database.

1. For each database server, what are the primary concerns relating to read performance, write performance, and disk storage?

    a. Production database:

    _____

    _____

    b. Decision support database:

    _____

    _____

2. When transferring records, what can you do to avoid write errors due to conflicting key values?

    _____

    _____

3. More data is collected during periodic data collection from the manufacturing line than can physically fit in a single database row. How can you resolve this problem?

    _____

    _____

4. What are the major influences on index design for each database?

    a. Production database:

    _____

    _____

b. Decision support database:

_____

_____

■ Part B: Case #2

An automotive parts chain has locations across the United States. Currently, the only automated database application is in the main office in Dallas, Texas. You are modifying the application design to support all locations.

Because of recognized differences in regional requirements, each location will have primary responsibility for its own inventory. A master inventory table, based on the inventory in each regional location, will be maintained in the main office in Dallas. There is also a supply warehouse in Dallas. Each office sends its inventory replacement orders to the Dallas warehouse. Orders to outside vendors must be placed from the Dallas warehouse.

Customer invoices post to both the local database and the master database in Dallas. Updates are not made unless they are successful in both locations. Customer records for business customers are also maintained in Dallas and in each location. Permanent customer information is not maintained for walk-in customers, just the walk-in invoices. In Dallas, walk-in invoices are tracked by location.

1. The current inventory table in Dallas will have the following columns: ItemSKU, Description, PrimaryVendor, AlternateVendor, QuantityOnHand, QuantityOnOrder, Cost, ListPrice, StandardPrice, and Status (as Valid, Do not order, or Discontinued).

    a. How will the inventory table be partitioned?

    _____

    _____

    b. How must you modify the master table to support partitioning?

    _____

    _____

    c. On what master table column(s) must you enforce uniqueness?

    _____

    _____

2. What is the minimum requirement for enforcing inventory entity integrity at each remote location?

_____

_____

3. You need to track sales by location, by quarter, and by item. You must accomplish this with minimal impact on storage requirements. How can you do this?

_____

_____

4. How can you ensure that invoice requirements are met?

_____

_____

5. What policy integrity requirements are defined in this scenario?

_____

_____

■ Part C: Case #3

You are working with a startup company that plans to do online sales. Customers will register with general information, including name, screen name, e-mail address, and a password of their own choice. They will use the screen name and password for login and e-mail address if they need to request a forgotten password.

Items for sale will have both an internally generated item ID value and a vendor part number. Items are offered by vendor. Some vendors offer duplicate items, and you found that some have duplicate part numbers. You want to limit the quantity on hand and restrict restocking levels on high-value items, based on your cost for the item. You plan to keep a short description (the item name) and a long description (full description of the item) for each item. During initial data entry, if you don't have a long description, you want to have "Description pending" entered in the field.

1. How can you automatically ensure that a customer doesn't pick a screen name that someone else is already using?

_____

_____

2. What's the easiest way to enforce minimum password length in the database?

_____

_____

3. What kind of database object can you use to ensure that programmers don't display more information out of the inventory than you want users to see?

_____

_____

4. What uniqueness constraints do you need to enforce on the inventory table?

_____

_____

5. What place, if any, should default constraints have in the design?

_____

_____

6. What should you use to enforce ordering limits on high-value items through the database?

_____

_____

Project 5.3	Creating a Database
Overview	The first step in physically implementing a database solution is creating the database. The database, in turn, contains database objects like tables, views, and indexes. Depending on your DBMS, you can do this using a command-line or GUI interface.
Outcomes	After completing this project, you will know how to: ▲ create a database in SQL Server ▲ view database properties
What you'll need	To complete this project, you will need: ▲ a computer with SQL Server 2005 Evaluation Edition installed
Completion time	15 minutes
Precautions	You should be logged in as an administrator during this project. Do not make changes to any database other than the one you are creating. You will be using this database in other Chapter 5 projects.

■ Part A: Create a destination folder

1. Open the **Start** menu and select **My Computer**.
2. Expand **Local Disk (C:)**.
3. Select **File**, click **New,** and then click **Folder**.
4. Enter **CH5Data** as the folder name and press the **Enter** key. **Note:** Do not close the **My Computer** window.

■ Part B: Create a database

1. To launch **SQL Server Management Studio**, open the **Start** menu, point to **All Programs**, select **SQL Server 2005**, and then click **SQL Server Management Studio**.
2. Click **Connect** to connect to your local server instance.
3. If not already expanded, expand your server instance in **Object Explorer**.
4. Right-click **Databases** and select **New Database**.
5. Type **Chap5** in the **Database name** field.
6. Scroll right until **Path** is visible under **Database files**.
7. Overwrite both path locations with **C:\CH5Data**, as shown in Figure 5-1.

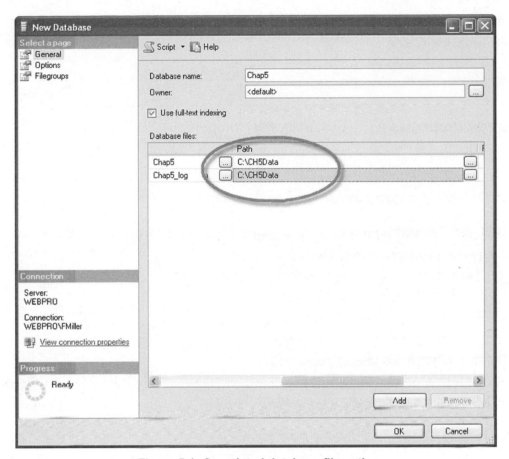

Figure 5-1: Completed database file paths

8. Under **Select a page**, click **Options**.

9. Review, but do not change, the database options.

10. Click **OK** to create the database.

■ Part C: Verify database creation

1. In the **My Computer** window, expand **CH5Data**. What files do you see listed?

    _____

    _____

2. What are potential disadvantages of putting all of the files of a database on the same physical hard disk?

    _____

    _____

3. Right-click **Chap5.mdf** and select **Properties**.
4. What is the file size?

_____

_____

5. Close the **Properties** dialog box and the **My Computer** window.

■ Part D: Verify database properties

1. In **SQL Server Management Studio**, under **Object Explorer**, expand **Databases**.
2. Locate, select, and then expand **Chap5**.
3. Select **Tables**. What do you see listed?

_____

_____

4. Right-click **Chap5** and select **Properties**.
5. Under **Select a page**, choose **Files** as shown in Figure 5-2. Verify that the file information is the same as specified when you created the database.

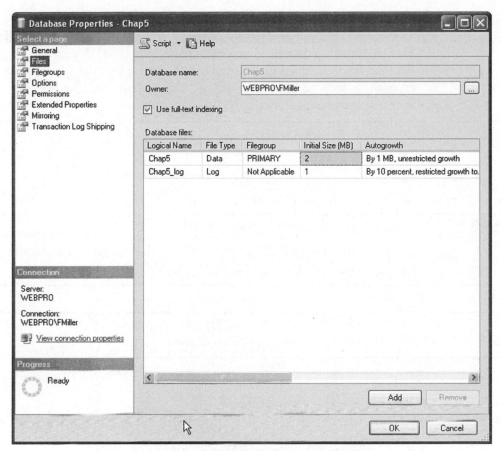

Figure 5-2: Database Properties dialog box

6. What is the initial database file size? How does this compare with the file size found in part C, step 4?

_____

_____

7. Select **Options**. These are the same options as you saw before.
8. Click **Cancel** to close the database **Properties** dialog box.

Project 5.4	Creating Tables, Part 1
Overview	One of your first database implementation tasks is to create database tables. Depending on the DBMS, you can use GUI-based utilities or create tables from the command line. Many people, especially when first learning database management, prefer GUI-based utilities.
Outcomes	After completing this project, you will know how to: ▲ create a table ▲ create an identity column ▲ create a foreign key relationship
What you'll need	To complete this project, you will need: ▲ a computer with SQL Server 2005 Evaluation Edition installed ▲ the database Chap5 created in Project 5.3
Completion time	30 minutes
Precautions	Do not make changes to any database other than Chap5. Do not make any changes other than those specified in this project.

■ Part A: Launch SQL Server Management Studio

1. If not already running, launch **SQL Server Management Studio** and connect to your local database server.
2. Locate and select the **Chap5** database.

■ Part B: Create the Office table

1. Right-click **Tables** and select **New Table**.
2. Create the table as follows:

Column Name	Data Type	Allow Nulls
OfficeNumber	int	Clear check
Extension	nchar(4)	Clear check
Size	int	Check

3. Right-click **OfficeNumber** and select **Set Primary Key**. What constraints, if any, does this place on OfficeNumber?

_____

_____

4. Open the **File** menu and select **Save Table_1**.

5. Type **Office** as the table name and click **OK**. Your table should look like the example in Figure 5-3.

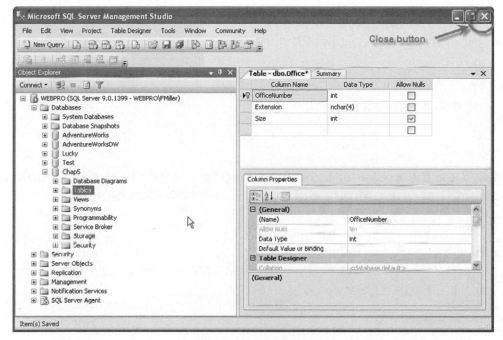

Figure 5-3: Finished table

6. Close the **dbo.Office** window. The **Close button (X)** is indicated in Figure 5-3.

■ Part C: Create the SalesPerson table

1. Right-click **Tables** and select **New Table**.

2. Create the table as follows:

Column Name	Data Type	Allow Nulls
EmpID	int	Clear check
SPNumber	nchar(4)	Clear check
FirstName	nvarchar(20)	Clear check
LastName	nvarchar(20)	Clear check
CommissionPercentage	real	Clear check
OfficeNumber	int	Check

3. Right-click **EmpID** and select **Set Primary Key**.
4. Open the **File** menu and select **Save Table_1**.
5. Type **SalesPerson** as the table name and click **OK**.
6. Close the **dbo.SalesPerson** window.

■ **Part D: Use the steps already described to create the Product table and set ProductID as the primary key, using the following columns:**

Column Name	Data Type	Allow Nulls
ProductID	int	Clear check
ProductNumber	nvarchar(20)	Clear check
Description	nvarchar(50)	Clear check
UnitPrice	money	Check
OnHand	int	Clear check

Project 5.5	Setting Table Constraints
Overview	When creating table columns, you are required to define the data type and nullability. Even if you don't specify values for these, they are set through the database and DBMS defaults. When you create tables, you will typically also need to define table and column constraints. Constraints help in enforcing entity, domain, and referential integrity. In some situations, they can also enforce policy integrity.
Outcomes	After completing this project, you will know how to: ▲ view table properties ▲ specify unique constraints ▲ specify default constraints ▲ specify referential constraints
What you'll need	To complete this project, you will need: ▲ a computer with SQL Server 2005 Evaluation Edition installed ▲ the database Chap5 created in Project 5.3 ▲ the tables you added in Project 5.4
Completion time	45 minutes
Precautions	Do not make changes to any database other than Chap5. Do not make any changes other than those specified in this project.

■ Part A: Launch SQL Server Management Studio

1. If not already running, launch **SQL Server Management Studio** and connect to your local database server.
2. Locate and expand the **Chap5** database.
3. Expand **Tables**.

■ Part B: View information about tables

1. Right-click **dbo.Office** and select **Properties**. Notice that the **Properties** dialog box provides technical and security information about the table, but nothing about the table design or columns.
2. Click **Cancel**.
3. Expand **dbo.Office**, and then expand **Columns**. Verify that the columns you specified are listed.
4. Expand **Indexes** as shown in Figure 5-4. The **PK_Office (Clustered)** index was created automatically when you set the table's primary key.

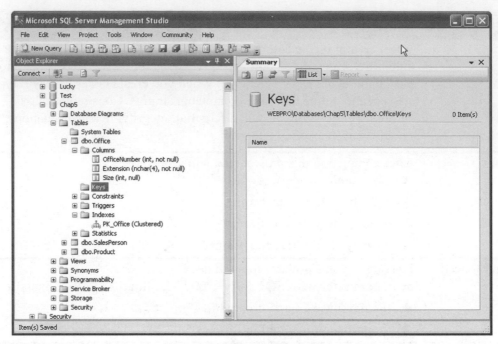

Figure 5-4: Office table indexes

5. What other indexes would you expect to find in the **Chap5** database at this time?

_____

_____

6. Verify your answers by checking the remaining tables.

■ **Part C: Complete the Office table**

1. Right-click **Office** and select **Modify**.
2. You want the office number created automatically, starting with 100. Select the **OfficeNumber** column.
3. Under **Column Properties**, locate and expand **Identity Specification**.
4. Set **(Is Identity)** to **Yes**, **Identity Increment** to **1**, and **Identity Seed** to **100**, as shown in Figure 5-5.

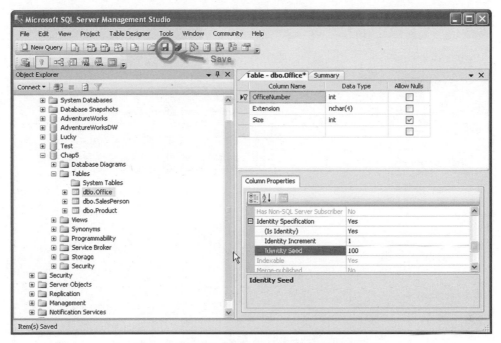

Figure 5-5: Office identity column settings

5. Click the **Save** toolbar button to save changes, and then close the modification window.

■ Part D: Complete the SalesPerson table

1. Right-click **SalesPerson** and select **Modify**.
2. Select **CommissionPercentage**.
3. Under **Column Properties**, locate **Default Value** or **Binding** and enter a value to **8.5**.
4. Remove the check under **Allow Nulls** for the **OfficeNumbe**r column.
5. Right-click **OfficeNumber** and select **Relationships.**
6. Click **Add**.
7. Click the browse button **(…)** to the right of **Tables and Columns Specification**.
8. Select **Office** as the **Primary key table**, and below the table selection, choose **OfficeNumber** from the drop-down list.
9. Verify that **SalesPerson** is the **Foreign key table**, and below the table selection, choose **OfficeNumber** from the drop-down list. Your **Tables and Columns** dialog box should look like Figure 5-6.

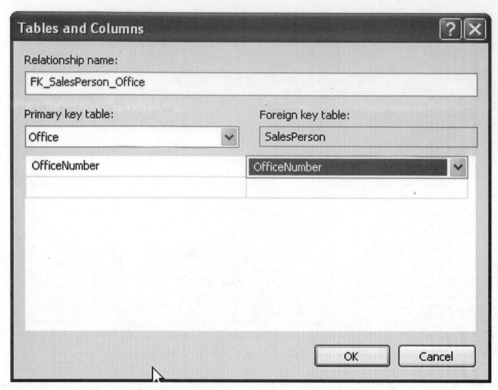

Figure 5-6: Tables and Columns selections

10. Click **OK** to close the **Tables and Columns** dialog box and **Close** to close the **Foreign Key Relationships** dialog box. What kind of integrity does this enforce?

_____

_____

11. Right-click **SPNumber** and select **Indexes/Keys**.
12. Click **Add**.
13. Click the **browse** button for **Columns**, choose **SPNumber**, and click **OK**.
14. From the **Is Unique** drop-down list, choose **Yes**. Your **Indexes/Keys** dialog box should look like Figure 5-7.

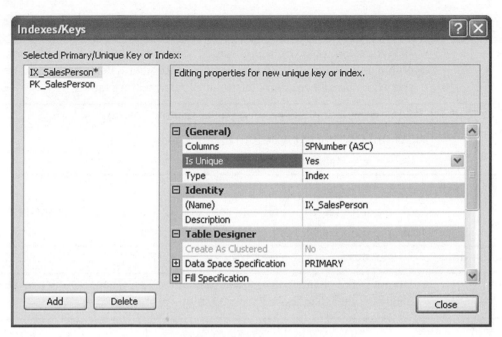

Figure 5-7: SalesPerson Indexes/Keys

15. Click **Close**.

16. Save your changes. When prompted to save changes to **Office** and **SalesPerson**, click **Yes**.

17. Close the **SalesPerson** modification window.

■ Part E: Finish the Product table

1. Using the steps previously described, open **Product** for modification.

2. Set the default for the **OnHand column** to **0 (zero)**.

3. Configure **ProductID** as an identity column with seed and increment values of **1**.

4. Save your changes.

■ Part F: Review your changes

1. Under each table, review the **Indexes**, **Keys**, and **Constraints** folders to see what is listed under each.

Project 5.6	Creating Tables, Part 2
Overview	In some situations, you might find it necessary to use command-line commands and utilities to create tables and other database objects. You can specify table and column constraints while creating tables.
Outcomes	After completing this project, you will know how to: ▲ use CREATE TABLE to create tables ▲ specify table constraints
What you'll need	To complete this project, you will need: ▲ a computer with SQL Server 2005 Evaluation Edition installed ▲ the database Chap5 created in Project 5.3
Completion time	30 minutes
Precautions	Do not make changes to any database other than Chap5. Do not make any changes other than those specified in this project.

■ Part A: Launch SQL Server Management Studio and open a query window

1. If not already running, launch **SQL Server Management Studio** and connect to your local database server.
2. Locate and expand the **Chap5** database.
3. Right-click **Chap5** and select **New Query**. **Chap5** should be the default database, as shown in Figure 5-8.

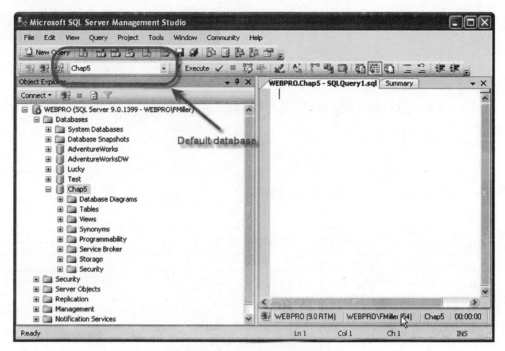

Figure 5-8: Default database

■ **Part B: Create the Customer table**

1. Type the following in the query window:

```
CREATE TABLE dbo.Customer
(CustomerNumber int IDENTITY(1,1)
PRIMARY KEY NONCLUSTERED,
CustomerName nvarchar(50) NOT NULL,
SalesPerson nchar(4) REFERENCES dbo.SalesPerson(SPNumber),
HQCity nvarchar(20) NOT NULL,
HQState nvarchar(2) NOT NULL)
```

2. Press **F5** to execute the command.
3. Answer the following questions about the **Customer** table:
   a. What is the primary key, if any?

   _____

   _____

b. What referential integrity, if any, is defined?

_____

_____

c. Why won't any columns accept NULL values?

_____

_____

d. What other constraints, if any, are defined?

_____

_____

■ Part C: Create the CustomerEmployee table

1. Press **CTRL+SHIFT+DEL** to clear the query window.
2. Type the following in the query window:

```
CREATE TABLE dbo.CustomerEmployee
(CustomerNumber int REFERENCES
dbo.Customer(CustomerNumber),
EmployeeNumber varchar(10) NOT NULL,
FirstName nvarchar(20) NOT NULL,
LastName nvarchar(20) NOT NULL,
Title nvarchar(50) DEFAULT 'Purchasing Employee',
Contact varchar(20) NULL)
```

3. Execute the query.
4. Answer the following questions about the **CustomerEmployee** table:
   a. What is the primary key, if any?

_____

_____

   b. What referential integrity, if any, is defined?

_____

_____

c. Which columns, if any, allow NULL values?

_____

_____

d. What other constraints, if any, are defined?

_____

_____

5. Close the query window. Click **No** when prompted to save changes.

■ Part D: Verify your new tables

1. Right-click **Tables** and select **Refresh**.
2. Expand tables, and then verify that **Customer** and **CustomerEmployee** are listed.
3. For each new table, expand the table, and then expand **Columns** and verify the column list.
4. Under **Customer**, expand **Keys**. You should see two keys, a primary key and a foreign key, listed.
5. Under **CustomerEmployee**, expand **Keys**. You should see one key, a foreign key, listed.
6. Check the contents of the **Indexes** and **Constraints** folders for each new table.

■ Part E: Modify the CustomerEmployee table

1. Right-click **CustomerEmployee** and select **Modify**.
2. Verify the column list to ensure that you see the column names and data types you specified.
3. Click **CustomerNumber**, hold the **SHIFT** key, and click **EmployeeNumber** so both columns are selected, and then right-click **EmployeeNumber** and select **Set Primary Key**. Your table should look like the example in Figure 5-9.

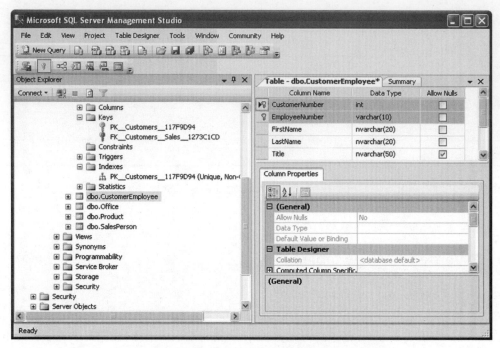

Figure 5-9: Modified CustomerEmployee table

4. On the toolbar, click **Save**. Why are you also prompted to save **Customer**?

_____

5. Click **Yes**.

6
UNDERSTANDING THE SQL LANGUAGE

PROJECTS

Project 6.1	Understanding Terms and Concepts
Overview	Implementing your database design includes selecting your DBMS and hardware platform, creating your databases, and creating your database objects. As with any other phase of the process, it is critical that you understand key terms and concepts.
Outcomes	After completing this project, you will know how to: ▲ identify key terms related to the SQL language ▲ identify key concepts related to SQL language command execution
What you'll need	To complete this project, you will need: ▲ the worksheet below
Completion time	20 minutes
Precautions	None

The worksheet below includes a list of items on the left and descriptions on the right. Match each term with the letter of its best description. You will use all descriptions. Each description can be used only once. The definitions used are based on ANSI standard SQL.

___ Minimally logged

___ Nonlogged

___ Query mode

___ Function

___ Embedded SQL

___ Qualifying condition

___ Parameter

___ Keyword

A. Operational mode where statements are executed through an interactive user interface for direct execution on the database server

B. Any set of executable statements

C. Referring to a function that might return different results even if called with the same arguments

D. Argument provided to help determine how a command runs

E. Ranking used to determine processing order

F. Situation where the fact that an operation ran is not logged and any changes made are written directly to the database

G. Referring to a function that always returns the same result if you pass the same arguments

H. Statements that are executed in the context of another programming language

____ Batch

____ Script

____ Explicit conversion

____ Implicit conversion

____ Deterministic

____ Nondeterministic

____ Precedence

I. Process of automatically converting data into a compatible type

J. Part of a command identifying a clause to either pass arguments or define command actions

K. Logical and conditional operators used to filter the rows processed by a command

L. Process of manually converting data

M. Situation where the fact that an operation ran is logged, but not the operation's effect

N. Set of executable statements that have been saved together as a file

O. Special executable designed to operate on data and return a result

Project 6.2	Identifying Help Resources
Overview	It is unrealistic to think you would ever memorize the complete SQL command set, including all parameters and keywords. It is even less likely that you could learn the entire proprietary command set offered by any DBMS. Things become even more complicated if you need to know how a vendor's implementation varies from standard SQL or from other vendors' language sets. The type and amount of help provided by a vendor can be critical. However, it doesn't do you much good if you don't know how to access it. You need to be aware of available resources and how to use the Internet to locate additional resources.
Outcomes	After completing this project, you will know how to: ▲ access help from SQL Server Management Studio ▲ access help from SQL Server Books Online ▲ use help documentation options ▲ search the Internet for SQL references
What you'll need	To complete this project, you will need: ▲ the worksheet below ▲ a computer with SQL Server 2005 Evaluation Edition installed ▲ access to the Internet, starting with step 4. If you do not have Internet access available, stop after you finish step 3
Completion time	30 minutes
Precautions	This project includes online access to the Internet to search for help resources. You may be unable to reach some resources if your Internet access is filtered or blocked. Also, when searching the Internet, there is always a risk that you might be directed to inappropriate content. Use your own discretion before investigating links provided by any search engine.

■ Part A: Compare local resources

1. To launch **SQL Server Management Studio**, open the **Start** menu, point to **All Programs**, select **SQL Server 2005**, and then click **SQL Server Management Studio**.
2. When prompted, click **Connect** to connect to the default local SQL Server instance.
3. Open the **Help** menu and select **Search**. This opens the online help system, as shown in Figure 6-1.

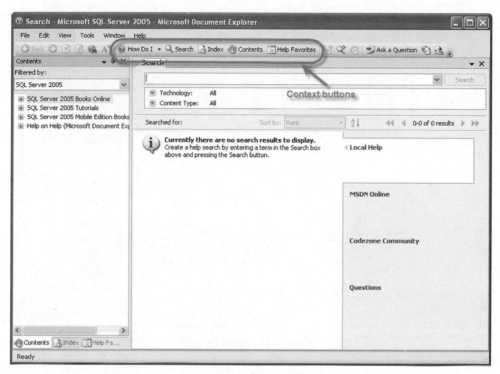

Figure 6-1: Help system

4. Click toolbar context buttons for **How Do I**, **Index**, **Contents**, and **Help Favorites** and compare the interface for each.

5. Open the **File** menu and select **Exit** to exit the help resources.

6. Open the **Start** menu, point to **All Programs**, select **Microsoft SQL Server 2005**, click **Documentation and Tutorials**, and then select **SQL Server Books Online**. This opens **Books Online**, as shown in Figure 6-2. Notice that the same toolbar context buttons are available as before. That is because this is a link to the same help system.

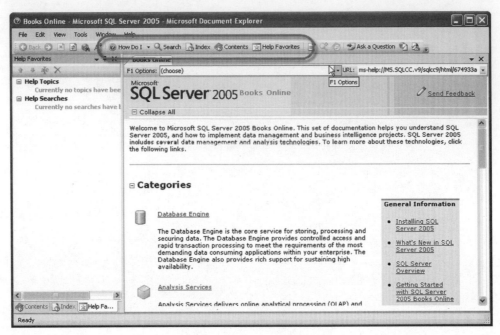

Figure 6-2: Books Online

7. Under **Categories**, click **Database Engine**. Review the information categories presented.

8. Exit **Books Online**.

■ Part B: Use local help resources

1. In **SQL Server Management Studio**, open the **Help** menu and select **Search**.

2. In the **Search** field, type **creating tables** and click **Search**.

3. If you have not configured **Help Settings**, you will be prompted to select whether to use online help or local help as the primary source. If you have Internet access, select **Use online Help as primary source** and click **OK**.

4. As shown in Figure 6-3, if you have Internet access and are currently connected, the help system automatically searches for additional help in **MSDN Online**, the **Codezone Community**, and **Questions**.

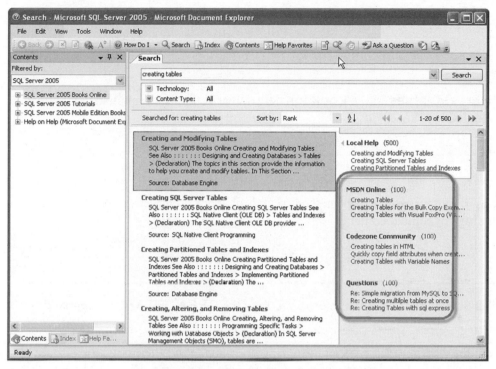

Figure 6-3: Suggested help topics

5. What is the first topic listed for local help?

_____

_____

6. Click the link. Does this topic apply to creating tables?

_____

_____

7. In the toolbar, click **Index**. In the **Look for** field, type **creating**. What is the first topic listed in the index list?

_____

_____

8. Now type **creating tables** in the **Look for** field. What is the first topic listed?

_____

_____

9. Click the link. Does this apply to creating tables?

_____

_____

10. Type **create tables** in the **Look for** field. What is the first topic listed, and does it apply to creating tables?

_____

_____

11. In this situation, which help method, search or index, returned a broader set of information including conceptual content?

_____

_____

12. Which help method took you more directly to the **CREATE TABLE** command?

_____

_____

13. From what you have seen, what can you say about the different help system contexts?

_____

_____

■ Part C: Find command syntax help

1. Click **Search** and search for **CREATE TABLE**. Find the **CREATE TABLE** statement in the topic list and click **CREATE TABLE(Transact SQL)**
2. Read the initial command syntax statement. Notice the use of syntax elements, such as italics and square brackets.
3. On the toolbar, click **Index**.
4. Type **Transact-SQL syntax**.
5. Click **Transact-SQL syntax conventions**. Two topics are found, as shown in Figure 6-4.

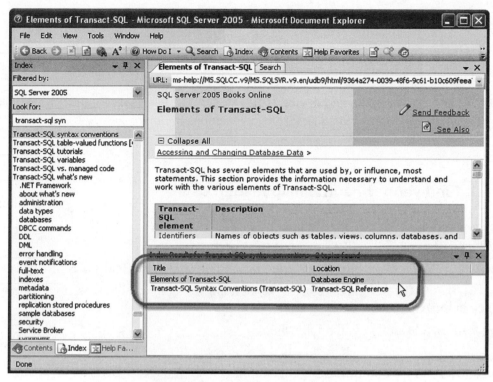

Figure 6-4: Multiple topics found

6. In the topic list, click **Transact-SQL Syntax Conventions (Transact-SQL)**. Review the syntax conventions and answer the following questions:

   a. How is italic type used?

   _____

   _____

   b. How is uppercase type used?

   _____

   _____

   c. How are optional syntax elements represented?

   _____

   _____

   d. How are required syntax elements represented?

   _____

   _____

e. What does it mean when something is enclosed in angle brackets.

_____

_____

f. Use the index to locate and open the CREATE TABLE syntax. Review the syntax again with what you've learned about syntax conventions in mind.

■ Part D: Find vendor-neutral help resources

1. Open your computer's Internet browser.
2. Navigate to the following URL: **www.google.com**
3. Type **ANSI SQL command help** in the search field and click **Google Search**.
4. Most of the URLs returned refer to vendor-specific implementations, even though you specified ANSI SQL.
5. Look for link title similar to the following:

   Google Directory - Computers > Programming > Languages > SQL

   If you find the link, click and view the contents. This is a list of more vendor-neutral resources. If time allows, investigate some of the links from this page.
6. If time allows, follow other command reference links to see what information they provide.

■ Part E: Find vendor-specific resources

1. Navigate to the following URL: **msdn.microsoft.com**
2. Find the list of topic areas and click **SQL Server**.
3. Explore the navigation menu to see the variety of reference information provided via the MSDN Web site.
4. Navigate to: **www.mysql.com**
5. Locate and click the **Documentation** link. This gives you an idea of how the volume of documentation for MySQL compares.

_____

_____

Project 6.3	Comparing Command Environments
Overview	SQL commands can be run interactively, in query mode, or embedded as part of another application. Even when you plan to use commands as embedded commands, you should first test them in query mode whenever possible to verify your command syntax and parameters. You have two basic options for interactive command execution. You can run them in a command-line environment or in a more graphical environment like the one provided through SQL Server Management Studio. It is best to be familiar with both.
Outcomes	After completing this project, you will know how to: ▲ run commands using the sqlcmd interface ▲ run commands through SQL Server Management Studio ▲ run commands through an operating system batch file
What you'll need	To complete this project, you will need: ▲ a computer with SQL Server 2005 Evaluation Edition installed
Completion time	30 minutes
Precautions	You should be logged in as an administrator during this project. Do not make changes to any database other than the one you are creating. You will be using this database in other Chapter 6 projects.

■ Part A: Create a working directory

1. Open the **My Computer** window.
2. Open the **C:** drive.
3. Open the **File** menu and select **New** and then **Folder**. Name the folder SqlTest.
   Note: You'll use this folder later in the project. Do not close the **My Computer** window.

■ Part B: Use a command-line interface

1. Open the **Start** menu, point to **All Programs**, point to **Accessories**, and select **Command Prompt** to open a **Command Prompt** window.
2. At the command prompt, type sqlcmd /? and press the **Enter** key.

3. Review the command options. Notice that the options are case sensitive. What is the option to connect using a trusted connection?

_____

_____

4. What is the option to specify an initial database?

_____

_____

5. At the command prompt, type `sqlcmd -E -dadventureworks` (see Figure 6-5), press the **Enter** key to open a connection to the local database server, and select the AdventureWorks database.

Figure 6-5: sqlcmd command prompt

6. Type `SELECT TOP 10 * FROM sales.customer` and then press the **Enter** key. What happens?

_____

_____

7. Type `go` and press the **Enter** key. What happens now?

_____

_____

8. After typing your commands, type `go` on a separate line to execute. Type the following and press the **Enter** key at the end of each line:

```
select top 2 * from people.contact
go
```

9. What happens?

_____

_____

10. Press the up arrow twice and backspace to erase `people.contact`, type `person.contact`, and execute the command. It should run without generating an error.

11. For each of the commands in Table 6-1, indicate whether the command returns an error when run:

Table 6-1: Sample commands

Command	Result
GETDATE()	
SELECT GETDATE()	
3 * 5 * 2	
SELECT 3 * 5 * 2	
CREATE DATABASE MYTEST	

12. To exit sqlcmd, type **exit** and press the **Enter** key. **Note:** Do not close the **Command Prompt** window.

■ Part C: Use a graphical interface

1. Launch **SQL Server Management Studio**.
2. Locate and expand **Databases**. Verify that you see **MYTEST** listed.
3. Right-click **AdventureWorks** and select **New Query**. This opens a query window as shown in Figure 6-6.

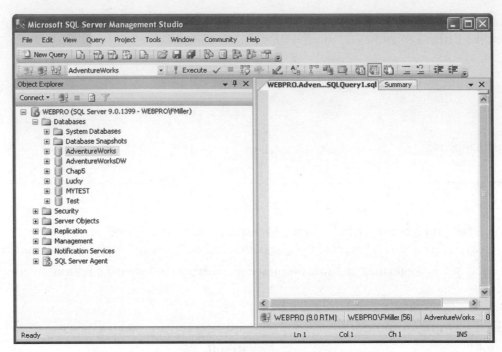

Figure 6-6: Query window

4. In the query window, type `SELECT TOP 2 FROM SALES.CUSTOMER`, then press the **Enter** key.

5. The command does not execute when you press the **Enter** key. Click **Execute** on the toolbar to see the result.

6. Click **Message**s to see any messages relating to the command.

7. Open the **Query** menu and select **Results to** and then **Results to Text**, and then click **Execute**. The result is now in a **Results** window, as shown in Figure 6-7.

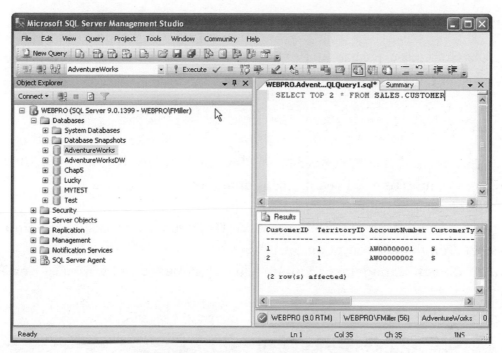

Figure 6-7: Using Results to Text

8. Execute the following: `select top 2 * from people.contact`. What happens?

_____

_____

9. Edit the line to replace `people` with `person` and execute the command. What happens?

_____

_____

10. Execute `DROP DATABASE MYTEST`. Refresh the **Databases** folder to verify that the database is not listed.

11. Test the commands in Table 6-1. How do the results compare to your initial test?

_____

_____

■ **Part D: Use an operating system batch file**

1. Open the **Start** menu, point to **All Programs**, point to **Accessories**, and click **Notepad**.
2. Type the following in **Notepad**:

```
sqlcmd -E -Q"CREATE DATABASE NEWTEST"
```

3. Open the **File** menu and select **Save As**. In **Save as Type** text box, select **All Files**.
4. Navigate to **C:\SqlTest** and save the file as **dbtest.bat**.
5. Exit **Notepad**.
6. In the **Command Prompt** window, type **C:\SqlTest\dbtest.bat** and press the **Enter** key.
7. Close the **Command Prompt** window.
8. In **SQL Server Management Studio**, refresh **Databases** and verify that **NewTest** is listed.

Project 6.4	Using the SELECT Command
Overview	The SELECT command is used to retrieve data and to evaluate expressions. In many applications, it is the most commonly used SQL command. Because of this, it's important that you be familiar and comfortable with the basic use and syntax of the SELECT command.
Outcomes	After completing this project, you will know how to: ▲ use SELECT to retrieve data from a table ▲ use SELECT to evaluate an expression
What you'll need	To complete this project, you will need: ▲ a computer with SQL Server 2005 Evaluation Edition installed ▲ the sample database Chapter6, which you will attach during this project
Completion time	30 minutes
Precautions	Do not make changes to any database other than Chapter6. Do not make any changes other than those specified in this project.

■ **Part A: If necessary, launch SQL Server Management Studio and connect to your local server**

■ **Part B: Attach the sample database**

1. Open the **My Computer** window and create a folder named **CH6Data** at the root of the **C:** drive.
2. Copy **CH6DB.zip** to **CH6Data** and extract the file to the default location.
3. In **SQL Server Management Studio**, right-click **Databases** and select **Attach**.
4. Click **Add**. Locate and select **C:\CH6Data\CH6DB\Chap6.mdf**, and then click **OK**.
5. In the **Attach Databases** dialog box, click **OK**.
6. Verify that the database **Chapter6** is listed. Expand **Chapter6**, and then expand **Tables**.

■ **Part C: Open a new query window and test**

1. Right-click **Chapter6** and select **New Query**.
2. Execute the following:

```
SELECT * FROM DBO.SALESPERSON
```

3. Verify that three rows are returned.

■ **Part D: Execute each of the queries below and describe the result**

Note: Clear the query window after executing each query.

1. SELECT * FROM DBO.SALESPERSON

    _____

    _____

2. SELECT * FROM OFFICE

    _____

    _____

3. SELECT * FROM DBO.CUSTOMER

    _____

    _____

4. SELECT FIRSTNAME, LASTNAME FROM SALESPERSON

_____

_____

5. SELECT FIRSTNAME + ' ' + LASTNAME AS
   [Full Name] FROM SALESPERSON

_____

_____

6. SELECT FIRSTNAME + ' ' + LASTNAME AS
   [Full Name] FROM SALESPERSON
   WHERE SPNUMBER = '3455'

_____

_____

7. SELECT FIRSTNAME + ' ' + LASTNAME AS
   [Full Name] FROM SALESPERSON
   WHERE SPNUMBER > '3455'

_____

_____

8. SELECT FIRSTNAME + ' ' + LASTNAME AS
   [Full Name] FROM SALESPERSON
   WHERE SPNUMBER >= '3455'

_____

_____

9. SELECT FIRSTNAME + ' ' + LASTNAME AS
   [Full Name] FROM SALESPERSON
   ORDER BY LastName

_____

_____

10. SELECT FIRSTNAME + ' ' + LASTNAME AS
    [Full Name] FROM SALESPERSON
    WHERE LastName Like 'D%'

_____

_____

11. `SELECT FIRSTNAME + ' ' + LASTNAME AS`
    `[Full Name] FROM SALESPERSON`
    `WHERE LastName Like '[^D]%'`

■ Part E: Resolve simple expressions

1. Resolve the expression **getdate()** by executing:

   `SELECT getdate()`

2. What is the result?

---

3. Try to guess the result in advance, and then resolve the expressions in Table 6-2. Describe the result returned by each expression:

Table 6-2: Expressions

Expression	Result
`SELECT 3*5+2*4`	
`SELECT 3*(5+2)*4`	
`SELECT 3*5+2+4`	
`SELECT 3*(5+2)+4`	
`SELECT 3*(5+2+4)`	
`SELECT 10/5*2`	
`SELECT 10/(5*2)`	
`SELECT COUNT(EmpID)` `FROM dbo.salesperson`	
`SELECT SUM(EmpID)` `FROM dbo.salesperson`	

Expression	Result
SELECT AVG(EmpID) FROM dbo.salesperson	
SELECT UPPER(FIRSTNAME + ' ' + LASTNAME) AS [Full Name] FROM SALESPERSON	
SELECT 10 + 3 SELECT 3 + 10	
SELECT 10%3 SELECT 3%10	
SELECT 10 * 3 SELECT 3 * 10	
SELECT 10/3 SELECT 3/10	

■ **Part F: View available functions**

1. Expand **Chapter6**, expand **Programmability**, **Functions**, and **System Functions**. How are the system functions organized?

   _____

   _____

2. Expand **Aggregate Functions**. Locate and expand **Count**, and then expand **Parameters**. What information do you get about the return value?

   _____

   _____

3. Expand **Date and Time Functions**, **Year()**, and **Parameters**.
   a. What type of parameter does **Year()** accept?

   _____

   _____

b. Hold the mouse pointer over **Year()**. What information is displayed in the **Tooltip**?

_____

_____

c. What data type is returned by **Year()**?

_____

_____

4. What could you run to get the year only from today's date?

_____

_____

5. Test you answer in the query window.
6. Expand each of the function categories and briefly review the functions supported for that type.
7. Collapse **Programmability**.

Project 6.5	Using DDL Commands
Overview	You use DDL commands to create and manage server and database objects. It's important that you understand their basic use. Once you've learned a few basic commands and their command syntax, it becomes easier to apply knowledge when you need to use other, more complicated DDL commands.
Outcomes	After completing this project, you will know how to: ▲ locate and use command syntax help ▲ create database objects ▲ modify database objects
What you'll need	To complete this project, you will need: ▲ a computer with SQL Server 2005 Evaluation Edition installed ▲ the sample database Chapter6 that you attached during Project 6.4
Completion time	45 minutes
Precautions	Do not make changes to any database other than Chapter6. Do not make any changes other than those specified in this project.

■ Part A: Launch SQL Server Management Studio and prepare to run commands

1. If not already running, launch **SQL Server Management Studio** and connect to your local SQL Server instance.
2. In **Object Explorer**, right-click your server instance and select **New Query**. Which database is selected by SQL Server as the default database?

   _____

   _____

■ Part B: View available DDL commands

1. Open the **Help** and select **Index**. Search the index for **CREATE**.
2. Scroll to view the variety of **CREATE** commands supported.
3. Search the index for **ALTER** and scroll through the commands. You should see a similar list.
4. Locate and select the **CREATE INDEX** command. Review the command syntax and relational options.
5. Locate and select the **ALTER INDEX** command. Review the command syntax. In general, how does the syntax compare to the **CREATE INDEX** command?

   _____

   _____

■ Part C: Create objects

1. Execute the following:

   ```
   use chapter6
   ```

2. What is the effect of this command?

   _____

   _____

3. Execute the following:

```
CREATE UNIQUE INDEX ix_SKU
ON dbo.product(productnumber)
```

4. In **Object Explorer**, expand **dbo.product**, right-click **Indexes**, and select **Refresh**.

5. Expand **Indexes** and locate **ix_SKU**.

6. Right-click **ix_SKU** and select **Script Index as,** then **CREATE To,** then click **New Query Editor Window**. This will open a new query window with a **CREATE INDEX** statement, as shown in Figure 6-8.

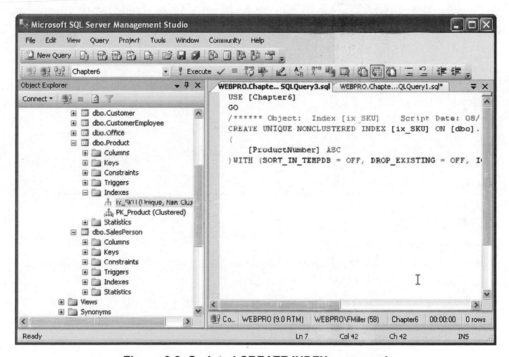

Figure 6-8: Scripted CREATE INDEX command

7. In general, how does this vary from the **CREATE INDEX** command string?

   _____

   _____

8. The additional parameter values are the default values at the time the index was created. Why would you want to script the statement with these values?

   _____

   _____

9. What is the value for **DROP_EXISTING**?

   _____

   _____

10. What is the syntax in this script for relational options (shown as **<relational_index_option>**)?

    _____

    _____

11. Close the query window containing the script.

12. Read through the **CREATE TABLE** syntax again. What would you run to create the following table, specifying required parameters only?

    Table name: dbo.Discount

    First column name: Customer

    First column type: int

    Second column name: Amount

    Second column type: real

    _____

    _____

13. Execute the command to test.

14. Refresh the **Tables** container, locate the table you just created, and script it to a query window. Compare the script to the command you ran.

15. What additional information about the columns is explicitly defined in the script?

    _____

    _____

16. You are going to create a view to limit access to the **SalesPerson** table. Execute the following:

```
CREATE VIEW v_Employee
AS (SELECT spnumber, firstname, lastname
FROM dbo.salesperson)
```

17. Execute the following to test:

```
SELECT * FROM v_Employee
```

18. Close the query window containing the script.

■ Part D: Modify and delete objects

1. You want to change **ix_SKU** to specify an included column. Execute the following:

```
CREATE UNIQUE INDEX ix_SKU
ON dbo.product(productnumber)
INCLUDE (Description)
```

2. What happens?

    _____

    _____

3. You could run DROP INDEX first, or modify the command. Execute the following:

```
CREATE UNIQUE INDEX ix_SKU
ON dbo.product(productnumber)
INCLUDE (Description)
WITH (DROP_EXISTING=ON)
```

4. You want to modify **dbo.Discount** to add a column. Execute the following:

```
ALTER TABLE dbo.Discount
ADD DateModified datetime DEFAULT getdate()
```

5. Review the ALTER TABLE syntax in the help files. What can you do in the ALTER COLUMN clause?

    _____

    _____

6. What statement would you run to delete **dbo.Discount**?

    _____

    _____

7. Execute the statement to test.

8. What statement would you run to drop **Chapter6**? (Do not run the command.)

_____

_____

9. Consider your current working environment. What conflicts might there be to dropping the database?

_____

_____

10. Close the query window. Do not save changes when prompted.

Project 6.6	Using DML Commands
Overview	In most databases, especially production databases, you will find it necessary to run DML statements on a regular basis. In most production databases, you are constantly adding, modifying, and deleting table rows. To support this, you need to understand the INSERT, UPDATE, and DELETE commands. For now, we will limit this to basic command use.
Outcomes	After completing this project, you will know how to: ▲ use INSERT to add rows to a table ▲ use UPDATE to add rows to a table ▲ use DELETE to remove rows from a table
What you'll need	To complete this project, you will need: ▲ a computer with SQL Server 2005 Evaluation Edition installed ▲ the database Chapter6
Completion time	30 minutes
Precautions	Do not make changes to any database other than Chapter6. Do not make any changes other than those specified in this project.

■ Part A: Launch SQL Server Management Studio and prepare to run commands

1. If not already running, launch **SQL Server Management Studio** and connect to your local SQL Server instance.
2. Locate and select the database **Chapter6**.
3. Right-click **Chapter6** and select **New Query**.

4. What is the advantage of right-clicking a specific database before running **New Query**?

_____

_____

■ Part B: Add data to tables

1. Execute the following:

```
SELECT * FROM office
```

2. Execute the following:

```
INSERT office (OfficeNumber, Extension, Size)
VALUES (110, 1101, 30)
```

3. What happens?

_____

_____

4. Execute the following statements as a set (a batch):

```
INSERT office (EXTENSION) VALUES (1422)
INSERT office (EXTENSION) VALUES (1422)
INSERT office (EXTENSION) VALUES (1219)
INSERT office (EXTENSION) VALUES (1220)
```

5. Execute the following to test:

```
SELECT * FROM office
```

a. How could you prevent the table from accepting duplicate values for **Extension**?

_____

_____

b. Why don't you need to provide values for **OfficeNumber** or **Size**?

_____

_____

6. Execute the following:

```
SELECT * FROM SalesPersons
```

7. Execute each of the following statements and describe the result.
   a. `INSERT salesperson`
      `VALUES (4, '2156', 'Jane', 'Doe', 9.0, 103)`

   _____

   _____

   b. `INSERT salesperson`
      `VALUES (5, '2209', 'Al', 'Thomas', DEFAULT, 104)`

   _____

   _____

   c. `INSERT salesperson`
      `VALUES (6, '2209', 'Bob', 'Roberts', DEFAULT, 105)`

   _____

   _____

   d. `INSERT salesperson`
      `VALUES (6, '2250', 'Bob', 'Roberts', DEFAULT, 110)`

   _____

   _____

   e. `INSERT salesperson`
      `VALUES (6, '2250', 'Bob', 'Roberts', DEFAULT, 106)`

   _____

   _____

8. Execute the following:

```
SELECT * FROM salesperson
```

9. Review the result set.

10. Execute the following:

```
SELECT * FROM v_Employee
```

11. Review the result set. Why does v_Employee include the new records when the view has not been modified?

_____

_____

■ Part C: Delete rows from tables

1. Execute the following:

```
DELETE office WHERE officenumber = 105
```

2. What happens?

_____

_____

3. Execute the commands in Table 6-3. Identify whether the command generates an error.

Table 6-3: Commands

Command	Result
DELETE office WHERE officenumber = 104	
DELETE office WHERE officenumber = 105	
DELETE office WHERE officenumber = 106	
DELETE office WHERE officenumber = 107	

4. What was the cause of the referential constraint errors.

   _____

   _____

5. Execute the following:

   ```
   SELECT * FROM office
   ```

6. What is the highest value for **OfficeNumber**?

   _____

   _____

7. Execute the following:

   ```
   INSERT office (EXTENSION) VALUES (2114)
   SELECT * FROM office
   ```

8. What **OfficeNumber** was assigned to the new office? Why?

   _____

   _____

7

DATA ACCESS AND MANIPULATION

PROJECTS

Project 7.1	Understanding Data Access
Overview	After you've deployed your database and any associated applications, nearly all activities related to the database will involved data access, data manipulation, or both. It's important to understand terms and concepts related to the activities.
Outcomes	After completing this project, you will know how to: ▲ identify key terms related to data access
What you'll need	To complete this project, you will need: ▲ the worksheet below
Completion time	20 minutes
Precautions	None

The worksheet includes a list of terms on the left and descriptions on the right. Match each term with the letter of its best description. You will use all descriptions. Each description can be used only once.

____ Search condition

A. Operators AND and OR used in filtering query results

____ Comparison operators

B. Expression that resolves as either true or false

____ Control statement

C. Query in which the result returns only qualifying rows from one table and all rows from a second table

____ Logical operator

D. Logical and comparison operators and values used to filter query results

____ Correlated subquery

E. Named set of executable statements that can be used as a query data source

____ Noncorrelated subquery

F. Query in which the result contains only qualifying rows from joined tables

____ Boolean expression

G. Database or database object name

____ Cartesian product

H. Object used to store a value temporarily in memory

____ Inner join

I. Query in which the inner query depends on values passed from the outer query

___ Outer join

J. Used in conditions to filter the results of a query, including =, >, <, >=, <=, <>, and !=

___ Table alias

K. Result returning all possible combinations of join columns

___ Local variable

L. Query in which the inner query does not depend on values passed from the outer query

___ User-defined function

M. Value used to replace and represent a table in a query

___ Identifier

N. Statements used to make decisions during batch execution and to manage batch execution

Project 7.2	Retrieving Data
Overview	The activity most often supported by many databases is data retrieval. Because of this, it's important to understand how to write and execute queries that retrieve data. Often, query requirements are specified by people who don't fully understand databases, or even the available data. Instead, they simply indicate the information that they want as a result.
Outcomes	After completing this project, you will know how to: ▲ retrieve specific rows and columns ▲ specify search conditions and filter results ▲ order query results ▲ combine query results
What you'll need	To complete this project, you will need: ▲ a computer with SQL Server 2005 Evaluation Edition installed ▲ to attach the database files for the Chapter 7 database. Create a folder named Chap7Data at the root of drive C: and copy the files GeneralHardware_new.mdf and GeneralHardware_log_new.ldf to that folder before starting this activity
Completion time	60 minutes
Precautions	Make sure that you are using the correct version of the GeneralHardware database. The activity results depend on having the correct database version.

■ Part A: Attach the database files for the Chapter 7 version of the GeneralHardware database

1. Open the **Start** menu, point to **All Programs**, point to **Microsoft SQL Server 2005**, and then select **SQL Server Management Studio**.
2. Click **Connect** to connect to the database server.
3. Right-click **Databases** in **Object Explorer** and select **Attach**.
4. Click **Add**.
5. Navigate to **C:\Chap7Data**, select **GeneralHardware_new.mdf**, and click **OK**.
6. Click **OK** to attach the database.
7. Expand **Databases**. You should see the database **Chapter7** listed as shown in Figure 7-1.

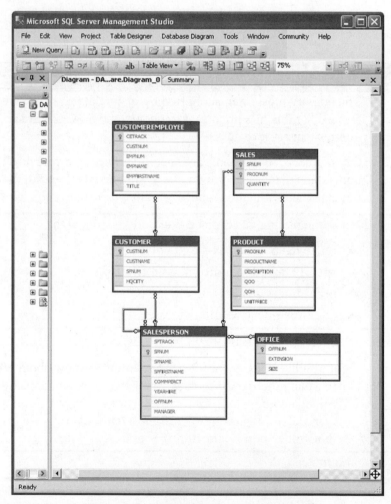

Figure 7-1: Attached Chapter7 database

8. Expand **Chapter7**, and then expand **Tables**. Review the tables in the **Chapter7** database.
9. Right-click **Chapter7** in **Object Explorer** and select **New Query** to open a new query window.

■ **Part B: For each of the following user data requests, create a query to retrieve the requested data. Record the query and the number of rows returned by the query**

1. "I need a list of all customer accounts that are headquartered in New York. I need the customer number and customer name. The order doesn't matter."

2. "Bring me a list of sales employees, first and last name only, in alphabetical order by last name."

3. "I want to see a list of sales employees hired after 1995. Include all information available about the employees."

4. "I want to see a list of sales employees hired since 1995, including that year. Include all information available about the employees."

5. "I want to know about product sales, by product. I just want to know about products, not who sold them. I need the product number and total sales for the top three items by quantity."

6. "Do salespersons 137 and 186 have any customers headquartered in the same city? If so, I just need the city."

_____

_____

_____

7. "Do salespersons 137 and 361 have any customers headquartered in the same city? If so, I just need the city."

_____

_____

_____

8. "I need a list of customer headquarter cities and the number of customers in each city. Give me the cities in alphabetic order."

_____

_____

_____

■ Part C: The following query requests are looking for a single result. For each request, provide the query used and the result

1. "What is the number of the salesperson who has sold the most of product number 16386?"

_____

_____

_____

2. "What is the full name of the VP of Sales for customer number 2198?"

_____

_____

_____

3. "What's the name of the salesperson with the lowest commission rate?"

    _____

    _____

    _____

4. "Salesperson 186 has a customer headquartered in a city in which salesperson 137 does NOT have any customers. What city is it?"

    _____

    _____

    _____

5. "Based on quantity, what's the product number of our best-selling product?"

    _____

    _____

    _____

6. "I want to know about sales for salesperson 137. Of the products for which that salesperson has recorded sales, which has the lowest quantity?"

    _____

    _____

    _____

Project 7.3	Using Advanced Data Retrieval
Overview	In a normalized database, many queries require you to retrieve data from multiple tables. The two most common ways of doing this are by using joins and subqueries. Because of resource requirements, when you have a choice, a join is usually the preferred of the two.
Outcomes	After completing this project, you will know how to: ▲ use joins to retrieve data ▲ use subqueries to retrieve data
What you'll need	To complete this project, you will need: ▲ a computer with SQL Server 2005 Evaluation Edition installed ▲ the Chapter7 database
Completion time	90 minutes
Precautions	None

■ **Part A: For each of the following user data requests, create a query to retrieve the requested data. Record the query and the number of rows returned by the query. When you have a choice, use joins instead of subqueries. You will need an open query window with Chapter7 selected as the default database**

1. "I want detailed sales records that include salesperson name, product number, and quantity sold. Rank the sales by quantity, lowest to highest."

_____

_____

_____

2. "I want a full list of customer names in customer number order. For each customer, I want the name of the assigned salesperson and the headquarters city."

_____

_____

_____

3. "I want a full list of customer names. For each customer, I want the name of the assigned salesperson. I also want the names and titles of any customer employees. I need this list in salesperson order, by name." (**Tip:** This requires an outer join.)

_____

_____

_____

4. Why does this query return more rows than the one in question 2?

_____

_____

_____

5. "I want a list of salespersons, last name only, and office sizes for each. I want the offices from smallest to largest."

_____

_____

_____

6. "Give me a list of customer names for customers who do not have employees on file."

_____

_____

_____

7. "I need a list of salesperson numbers with the number of customers assigned to each. Include all salespersons and label the count as 'Total'."

_____

_____

_____

8. "Get me an alphabetical company phone list – Name, Office number, and Extension. Make sure that they're labeled that way, too!"

_____

_____

_____

■ Part B: The following query requests are looking for a single result. For each request, provide the query used and the result

1. "What is the name of the salesperson who has sold the most, by total quantity?" (Use a subquery to retrieve this result.)

_____

_____

_____

2. "What is the name of Mark Adam's customer in Chicago?"

_____

_____

_____

3. "What's the name of the product having the most sales?"

_____

_____

_____

■ Part C: Rewrite the query to use a subquery

1. "Who sold the most electric drills? I want a name!" (Use two nested subqueries. Use the PRODUCT DESCRIPTION of "Electric Drill" in the innermost subquery.)

_____

_____

_____

2. Rewrite this as a join.

_____

_____

_____

Project 7.4	Using Batches and Scripts
Overview	You might find it easier to manage some periodic activities by creating a batch to perform the operations for you. A batch is one or more statements that execute as a group. You can include control-of-flow statements in your batch to make decisions while it is running. A script is a file containing one or more batches. You can save a script, and then retrieve it later for execution.
Outcomes	After completing this project, you will know how to: ▲ write and test batches ▲ write and test scripts
What you'll need	To complete this project, you will need: ▲ a computer with SQL Server 2005 Evaluation Edition installed ▲ the Chapter7 database ▲ an open query window
Completion time	30 minutes
Precautions	Don't worry about the default database at this point.

■ Part A: Create working tables

You will create a set of working tables based on your database tables. In some cases, you will be provided with the query to use to create the table.

1. Select **Chapter7** as the default database.
2. Run the following query:

```
SELECT * INTO WORKEMP FROM SALESPERSON
```

3. Run a query to create a table named WORKCUST using rows and columns from CUSTOMER.
4. Run a query to create a table named WORKSALES using rows and columns from SALES.
5. Run the following query:

```
SELECT PRODNUM, PRODUCTNAME, QOH, UNITPRICE,
(UNITPRICE * QOH) AS [VALUE]
INTO PRODWITHVAL FROM PRODUCT
```

  a. What should this batch accomplish?

  _____

  _____

  b. Execute the batch and verify the result.

  _____

  _____

■ Part B: Create and test a batch

1. Type the following in the query window (exactly as written):

```
USE Chapter7
GO
DROP TABLE WORKEMP
DROP TABLE WORKCUST
DROP TABLE WORKSALE
GO
```

2. What should happen when you execute the batch? Explain your answer.

  _____

  _____

  _____

3. Execute the batch and test. Compare the actual result to your expected result.

  _____

  _____

■ **Part C: Modify a batch to correct errors, then save and execute a script**

1. Clear the query window and type the following:

```
USE Chapter7
DECLARE @VAL INT
SET @VAL = (SELECT COUNT(*) FROM PRODWITHVAL)
GO
IF @VAL >= 7
PRINT 'All there!'
ELSE
PRINT 'Something is missing'
GO
```

2. Execute the statements. What happens?

   _____

   _____

   _____

3. An error occurs because the scope of a local variable is limited to the batch in which it is
   created. Modify the batch so it will run without generating an error and print the string "All
   there!" in the result pane. Execute and test the result.

   _____

   _____

■ **Part D: Open the File menu and select Save SQLQuery1.sql As**

1. Navigate to **C:\Ch7Data your destination**.
2. Name the file **ProdVal.sql** and click **Save**.
3. Close the query window and do not save changes when prompted. Open a new query window
   with **Chapter7** as the default database and execute a statement to delete all rows from
   PRODWITHVAL that have a PRODNUM value greater than 20000. How many rows are
   deleted? (Write the query you use below.)

   _____

   _____

   _____

4. Close the query window, do not save changes when prompted, and open the **File** menu and then select **Open**, and then **File**.

5. Locate and select **ProdVal**, and then click **Open**. Click **Connect** when prompted. What happens?

_____

_____

_____

6. Execute the contents of the query window. What happens? Explain the result.

_____

_____

_____

Project 7.5	Recognizing and Correcting Syntax Errors
Overview	Mistakes are common when first learning a new language. Syntax errors are easy to make and can result from not completely understanding a command, using clauses in the wrong order, using quotes improperly, and other similar mistakes. In many cases (or in most as you get more experienced), the errors are simple typing mistakes.
	Although not a big issue when working interactively (in a query window, unless you delete the wrong thing), syntax errors can be frustrating when used in dynamic SQL implementations. This is especially true when you have a logical error, rather than a syntax error. In other words, the command runs but produces the wrong result.
Outcomes	After completing this project, you will know how to: ▲ recognize statement errors ▲ correct detected errors
What you'll need	To complete this project, you will need: ▲ a computer with SQL Server 2005 Evaluation Edition installed ▲ the Chapter7 database
Completion time	20 minutes
Precautions	None

■ **Part A: You will be given a requested result and a query statement. For each, identify whether the statement contains an error. If the statement contains an error, explain what is wrong, write the corrected statement as indicated, and then test to ensure that you receive the correct result**

(**Tip:** If you're having problems correcting a query, try running it and see if the error message returned, if any, provides any help.)

1. "I want to see a list of sales employees hired after 1995. Include all information available about the employees."

   Original query:

   ```
   SELECT * FROM SALESPERSON
   WHERE YEARHIRE >= 1995
   ```

   a. Contains error?

   _____

   _____

   b. Corrected query:

   _____

   _____

2. "Give me a list of product sales by quantity. I want totals and product names only. The order doesn't matter."

   Original query:

   ```
   SELECT SUM(QUANTITY), PRONAME FROM SALES, PRODUCT
   WHERE SALES.PRODNUM = PRODUCT.PRODNUM
   GROUP BY PRODNUM
   ```

   a. Contains error?

   _____

   _____

b. Corrected query:

_____

_____

3. "How many different products has each salesperson sold? By salesperson number is okay, and just include the people with sales."

Original query:

```
SELECT SPNUM, COUNT(PRODNUM) FROM SALES
GROUP BY SPNUM
```

a. Contains error?

_____

_____

b. Corrected query:

_____

_____

4. "I want a list of salespersons in office number order. Include the office number, name, and office size." (**Tip:** You should enclose SIZE in square brackets because SQL Server treats it as a reserved word. Check the tables for the correct column names.)

Original query:

```
SELECT SALESPERSON.OFFNUM, SPFIRSTNAME, SPNAME, [SIZE]
FROM OFFICE JOIN SALESPERSON
ON (SALESPERSON.SPNUM = OFFICE.SPNUM)
```

a. Contains error?

_____

_____

b. Corrected query:

_____

_____

5. "I want a ranking of wrench sales by person, lowest to highest, and include the number sold. Use the person's full name and label it that way." (**Tip:** Check the table for the correct product name.)

Original query:

```
SELECT SPFIRSTNAME + ' ' + SPNAME AS [Full Name],
QUANTITY FROM SALESPERSON, SALES
WHERE PRODNUM = (
SELECT PRODNUM FROM PRODUCT
WHERE PRODUCTNAME = 'Wrench')
AND SP.SPNUM = S.SPNUM
ORDER BY QUANTITY
```

a. Contains error?

_____

_____

b. Corrected query:

_____

_____

8

IMPROVING DATA ACCESS

PROJECTS

Project 8.1	Understanding Database Monitoring and Optimization
Overview	After you've deployed your database and any associated applications, nearly all activities related to the database will involve data access to either read or write data. Because of this, tuning database and server performance is an ongoing task. As data sets become larger and databases more active, optimizing data access becomes a critical function. Another issue, just as important, is controlling access to data. One way to do this is to isolate data tables from users instead of giving users direct access. When discussing data access control and optimization, it's important that you understand related terms and concepts.
Outcomes	After completing this project, you will know how to: ▲ identify key terms related to database and server monitoring ▲ identify key terms related to optimization and performance tuning
What you'll need	To complete this project, you will need: ▲ the worksheet below
Completion time	20 minutes
Precautions	None

The worksheet below includes a list of terms on the left and descriptions on the right. Match each term with the description that it most closely matches. You will use all descriptions. Each description can be used only once.

_____ Key column

_____ Alert

_____ Merged scan join

_____ Merged loop join

_____ Disk queue

_____ Bottleneck

A. Algorithm used to combine results from two tables by looping through a Cartesian product

B. Program designed to retrieve data about a specific aspect of system or application performance

C. Any condition that adversely affects performance

D. Named set of executable statements that can accept one or more input parameters and return a specific type of value

E. Area of disk storage set aside for use as system memory

F. Value returned by a procedure

____ Input parameter

G. Temporary data storage area set aside in memory

____ Output parameter

H. Named set of executable statements that supports both input and output parameters

____ Performance counter

I. Method for monitoring and responding to a performance threshold

____ Performance object

J. Set value that indicates a possible performance problem when exceeded

____ Paging file

K. Data value provided to a function or procedure

____ Cache

L. Group of related programs that retrieve information about performance

____ Procedure

M. Algorithm used to combine results from two tables that requires either sorted or indexed columns in common

____ Function

N. Configuration settings relating to multiple processor use

____ Threshold value

O. Column used to define index sort order

____ Processor affinity

P. Hard disk requests waiting to be resolved

Project 8.2	Investigating Resources and Configuration Settings
Overview	Performance is directly related to hardware resources and their availability. DBMS manufacturers provide you with minimum requirements, but these are not sufficient to meet the needs of most applications. However, before considering what changes you need to make, determine what you have available. Configuration settings can directly impact database server performance. Even if your computer has sufficient resources, database server and operating system configuration numbers can cause a server to exhibit less than optimal performance.
Outcomes	After completing this project, you will know how to: ▲ view Windows configuration settings ▲ view SQL Server configuration settings
What you'll need	To complete this project, you will need: ▲ a computer with SQL Server 2005 Evaluation Edition ▲ the sample database files for this chapter. Create a folder named Chap8Data at the root of drive C: and copy GeneralHardware_8.mdf and GeneralHardware_8.ldf to that folder
Completion time	45 minutes
Precautions	The goal in this project is to view configuration settings only. Do not modify the configuration settings.

■ Part A: Prepare a sample database

You will be using a version of the GeneralHardware database specifically designed for use with the projects in this chapter.

1. Open the **Start** menu, point **to All Programs**, point to **Microsoft SQL Server 2005**, and select **SQL Server Management Studio**.
2. Click **Connect** to connect to the database server.
3. Right-click **Databases** in **Object Explorer** and select **Attach**.
4. Click **Add**.
5. Navigate to **C:\Chap8Data**, select **GeneralHardware_8.mdf**, and click **OK**.
6. Click **OK** to attach the database.
7. Expand **Databases**. You should see the database **Chapter8** listed.

■ Part B: View available hardware resources

We'll start with ways to view available hardware resources. The steps provided here are specific to Windows XP. The same configuration settings are available in most other Windows versions, although some of the steps to view and modify these settings may vary.

1. Open the **Control Panel**.

2. If the **Control Panel** is in **Category View**, click **Switch to Classic View**, as shown in Figure 8-1.

Figure 8-1: Control Panel classic view

3. Double-click **System** to open the **System Properties** dialog box. What information about hardware and software is available?

_____

_____

_____

4. How much RAM memory is installed on your computer?

_____

5. Click the **Hardware** tab to view hardware properties.

6. Click **Device Manager**. A sample Device Manager result is shown in Figure 8-2.

Figure 8-2: Device Manager (sample)

7. Expand **Disk drives** to see how many disk drives are installed. What other information is provided?

    _____

    _____

8. Expand **Processors**. What information is provided?

    _____

    _____

9. Open the **File** menu and select **Exit** to close **Device Manager**.

10. Click **Cancel** to close the **System Properties** dialog box.

11. In the **Control Panel**, double-click **Administrative Tools**.

12. Double-click **Computer Management** to open the **Computer Management** console shown in Figure 8-3.

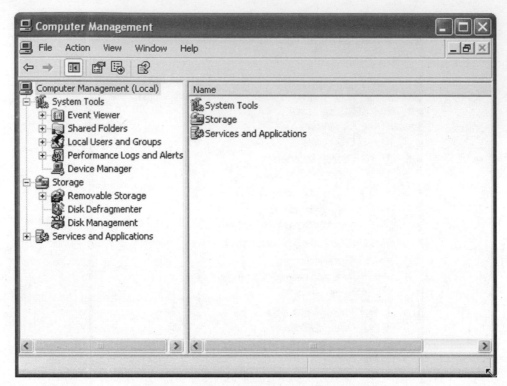

Figure 8-3: Computer Management console

13. Under **Storage**, select **Disk Management**. **Disk Management** displays hard disk and removable media, including file systems, disk status, and logical drive configuration. In Figure 8-4, you can see drive 1 configured as two logical drives.

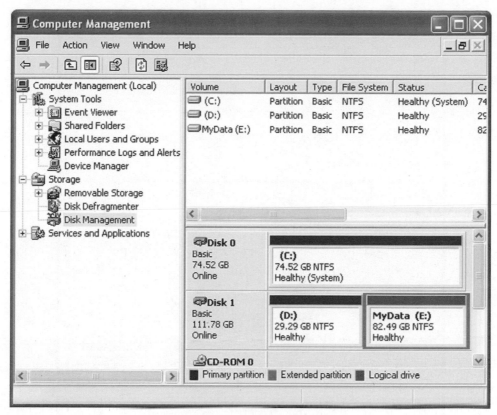

Figure 8-4: Disk Management

14. How many hard disks do you have?

_____

15. How many logical drives do you have?

_____

16. **Disk Management** shows you the total disk size. Right-click a logical disk and select **Properties** to display the **Disk Properties** dialog box, as shown in Figure 8-5. As you can see, the **General** tab in the **Disk Properties** dialog box reports disk size and available disk space.

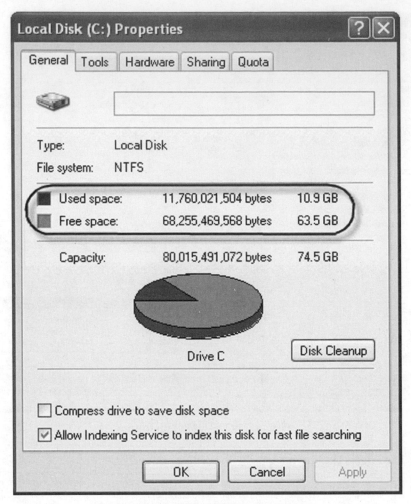

Figure 8-5: Disk Properties dialog box

17. Click **Cancel** to close the **Disk Properties** dialog box.

18. Close the **Computer Management** console, and then close the **Administrative Tools** window.

■ Part C: Windows configuration

Now we'll look at hardware configuration settings managed through the Windows operating system. The steps provided here are specific to Windows XP. The same configuration settings are available in most other Windows versions, although some of the steps to view and modify these settings may vary.

1. Open the **Control Panel**. Open the **System Properties** dialog box and click the **Advanced** tab.

2. Click **Settings**. The **Performance Options** dialog box opens. The **Visual Effects** tab lets you adjust visual effects for performance and appearance. Which default setting provides the best performance for a computer supporting a server application, such as SQL Server 2005?

_____

3. Click the **Advanced** tab. What performance settings are available on this page?

_____

4. Click **Change**, as shown in Figure 8-6, to manage virtual memory settings.

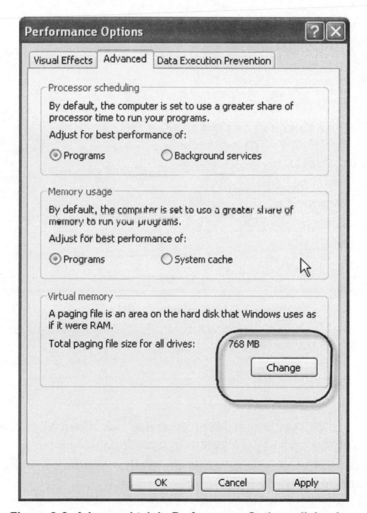

Figure 8-6: Advanced tab in Performance Options dialog box

5. Figure 8-7 shows sample virtual memory settings. For each logical drive, you can manually configure the paging file size, let Windows manage the size automatically, or specify that the drive should not have a paging file. In Figure 8-7, what is the maximum paging file size?

_____

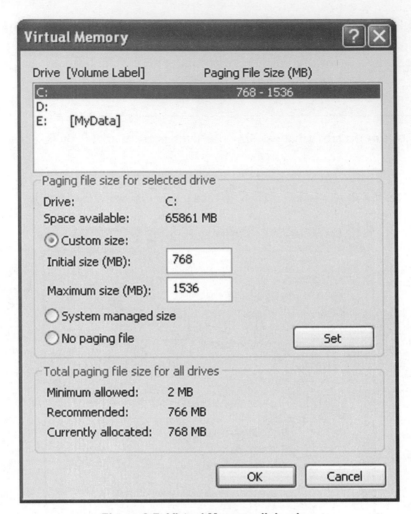

Figure 8-7: Virtual Memory dialog box

6. How does Windows use the paging file?

_____

_____

7. Click **Cancel** to close the **Virtual Memory** dialog box, **Cancel** to close **Performance Options**, and **Cancel** to close the **System Properties** dialog box.

8. In the **Control Panel**, open the **Administrative Tools** window and launch the **Computer Management** console.

9. Select **Device Manager**. Expand **Disk Drives**, right-click a disk drive, and select **Properties**.

10. Select the **Policies** tab, as shown in Figure 8-8. The option to enable write caching is enabled. Do not enable write caching on hard disks unless the controller is designed for use with a DBMS. Otherwise, data errors can occur after power outage or equipment failure.

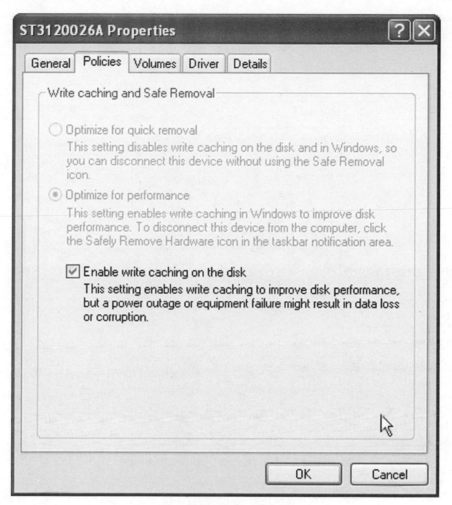

Figure 8-8: Policies tab

11. Click **Cancel** and exit the **Administrative Tools** window.

■ Part D: SQL Server configuration

SQL Server 2005 has a large number of configuration settings that can impact performance. These settings include server-level and database-level configuration settings.

1. Open **SQL Server Management Studio**. If prompted to connect, click **Connect**.

2. In **Object Explorer**, right-click your computer and select **Properties**.

3. Select **Memory**. This is where you manage the memory allocated to SQL Server, as shown in Figure 8-9.

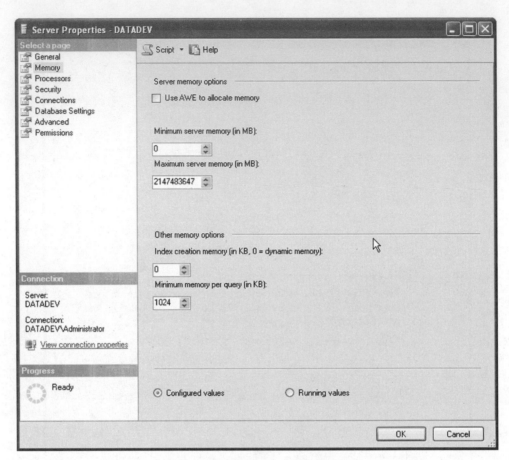

Figure 8-9: Memory configuration

4. How might increasing the minimum memory per query adversely impact system performance?

_____

_____

5. Select **Processors**, as shown in Figure 8-10. You can manage processor affinity, threads, and SQL Server priority through these settings.

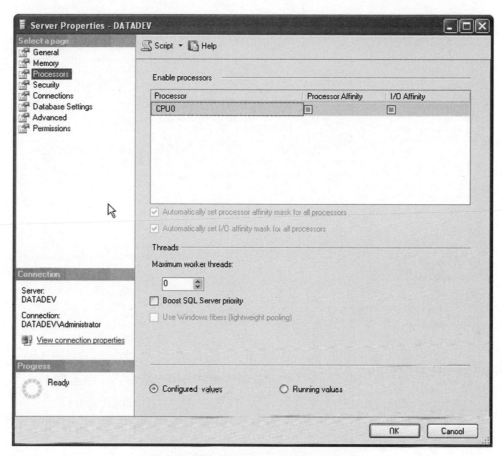

Figure 8-10: Processor configuration

6. In Figure 8-10, why are processor affinity options disabled?

    _____

    _____

7. Click **Cancel**.

8. Expand **Databases**, right-click **Chapter8**, and select **Properties**.

9. Select **Files**. This is where you manage database files. Scroll the properties until "**Path**" is available as shown in Figure 8-11.

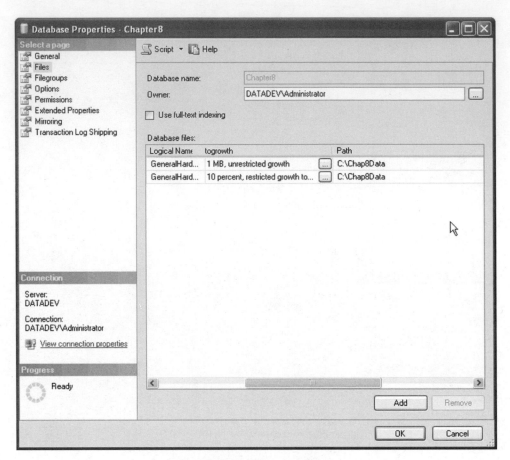

Figure 8-11: File properties

10. Click **Add**. What is the default file path?

_____

11. How would you create this file on a different hard disk?

_____

12. Click **Cancel** to close the properties without creating the new file.

13. Exit **SQL Server Management Studio**.

Project 8.3	Monitoring Performance
Overview	The tools available for monitoring performance depend on the operating system and DBMS. You need to understand the available monitoring tools so you know your options for monitoring system activity. Monitoring options include real-time monitoring, performance logging, and alerts.
	SQL Server 2005 also provides a variety of monitoring tools. The tools you use depend on the information you want to collect.
Outcomes	After completing this project, you will know how to:
	▲ monitor real-time system activity
	▲ collect a performance log
	▲ create an alert
	▲ monitor SQL Server activity
What you'll need	To complete this project, you will need:
	▲ a computer with SQL Server 2005 Evaluation Edition installed
	▲ the sample database files for this chapter. If you have not already done so, create a folder named Chap8Data at the root of drive C: and copy GeneralHardware_8.mdf and GeneralHardware_8.ldf to that folder
Completion time	60 minutes
Precautions	Do not run any queries that modify data other than those explicitly called for in this project.

■ Part A: Use Windows tools

You use the Performance utility to monitor performance. Monitoring options include real-time monitoring, logging, and alerts.

1. Launch the **Control Panel** and open the **Administrative Tools** window.
2. Double-click **Performance**. This opens the **Performance** utility with **System Monitor** open in the chart view, which is the default view, as shown in Figure 8-12.

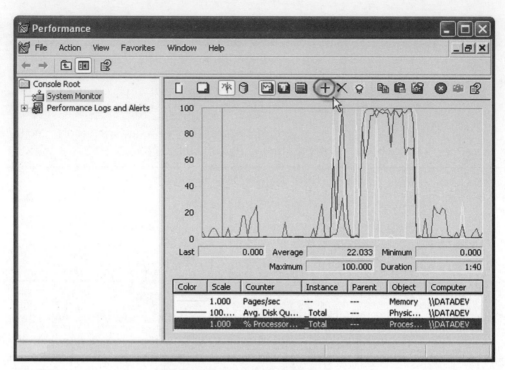

Figure 8-12: System Monitor

3. Click the **Add button (+)** to open the **Add Counters** dialog box. This lets you choose performance objects and counters.

4. Choose the **Memory** performance object and **Pages/sec** performance counter, as shown in Figure 8-13.

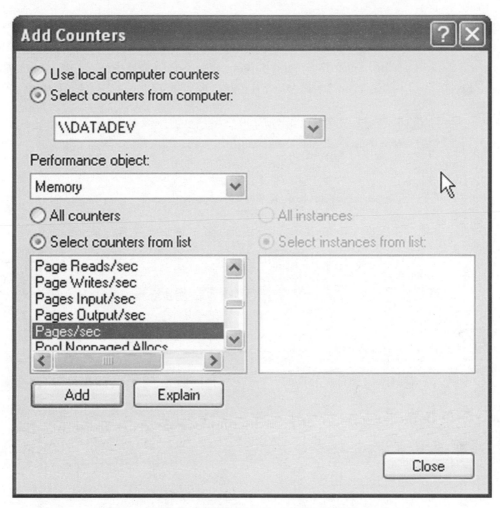

Figure 8-13: Select performance object and counter

5. Click **Add.** What happens?

_____

6   Click **Explain**. What happens?

_____

7. Select the **PagingFile** object. What counters are available?

_____

8. Click **Close**.
9. Launch **SQL Server Management Studio**. What happens in **System Monitor**?

_____

10. Expand **Performance Logs and Alerts**, then right-click **Alerts** and select **New Alert Settings**.

11. Name the alert **Proc Watch** and click **OK**.

12. Click **Add**.

13. Leave the default performance object and counter selected, click **Add**, and then click **Close**.

14. Set the **Over** limit at **95**. Your **Proc Watch** dialog box should look like Figure 8-14.

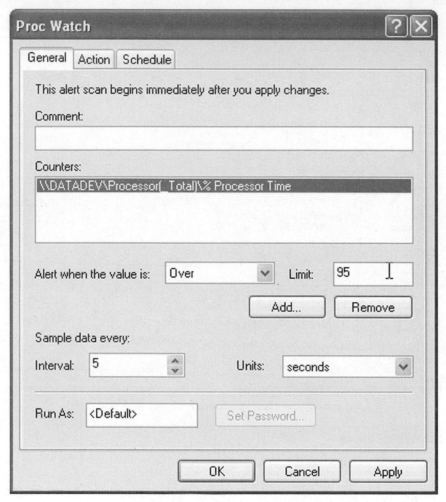

Figure 8-14: Proc Watch dialog box

15. Select **Action**. Review the available actions, then click **OK** to create the alert.

16. Select **Alerts** if it is not selected. What color is the **Proc Watch** icon?

_____

17. Right-click the alert and select **Stop**. What color is the icon now?

_____

18. Right-click the alert and select **Start**. What does the icon color tell you?

_____

19. Right-click **Counter Logs** and select **New Log Settings**. Name the log **SQL Test** and click **OK**.

20. Click **Add Counters**. Add the counters listed in Table 8-1.

Table 8-1: Performance objects and counters

Performance Object	Performance Counter	Instance
Processor	%Processor Time	Total
Memory	Pages/sec	N/A
Physical Disk	Current Disk Queue Length	0 C:
Physical Disk	Disk Bytes/sec	_Total
SQL Server:Buffer Manager	Buffer cache hit ratio	N/A

21. Click **Close** after adding the counters. Leave the remaining settings at their default values.

22. Select **Log Files** to configure the log file.

23. Click **Configure**. What is the default file location?

_____

24. Click **OK**. When prompted to create the folder, click **Yes**.

25. Click **Schedule**. Under **Start Log**, choose **Manually**.

26. Click **OK** to create the log.

27. Select **Counter Logs** and verify that SQL Test is listed. *Do not exit the Performance Utility!*

■ Part B: Use SQL Server tools

1. In **SQL Server Management Studio**, expand **Management** in **Object Explorer**.

2. Right-click **Activity Monitor** and choose **View Processes**. This will show the processes currently running on the server. How many items are listed?

_____

3. In **SQL Server Management Studio**, open a new query window.

4. In the **Activity Monitor** window, click **Refresh** as indicated in Figure 8-15.

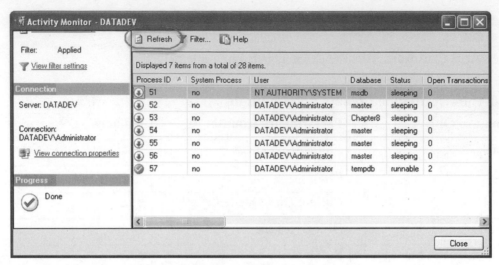

Figure 8-15: Activity Monitor

5.   What happens to the list of processes?

_____

6.   Click **Close** to close **Activity Monitor**.

7.   In **SQL Server Management Studio Object Explorer**, expand **SQL Server Agent**. **NOTE:** If it is not already running, you will be prompted to start SQL Server Agent. Start the agent, and then expand.

8.   Right-click **Alerts** and select **New Alert**. What type of events can you monitor?

_____

9.   Select **SQL Server performance condition alert**. Open the **Object** drop-down list. How does this list compare to the performance objects you saw in the **Performance** utility?

_____

10. Click **Cancel** to close the dialog box without creating an alert.

11. Open the **Start** menu, point to **All Programs**, point to **Microsoft SQL Server 2005**, select **Performance Tools**, and then select **SQL Server Profiler**. The **SQL Server Profiler** lets you capture SQL Server activity.

12. Open the **File** menu and select **New Trace**. Click **Connect** when prompted to connect to your database server.

13. Name the trace **ComboTest**.

14. Check **Save to Table** and click **Connect** when prompted. You are saving the data collected to a SQL Server table.

15. Choose **Chapter8** as the database and click **OK**.

16. DO NOT click **Run** at this time. Leave the remaining selections at default. Your trace should look like Figure 8-16.

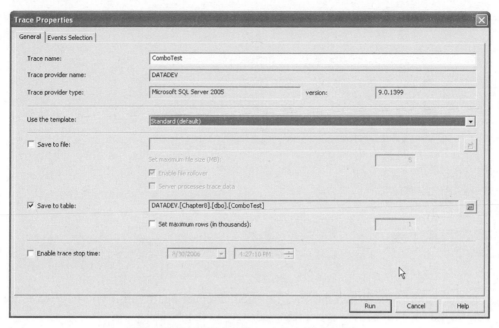

Figure 8-16: Trace Properties dialog box

17. *Do not exit any running utilities*.

■ Part C: Putting It together

Monitoring utilities in SQL Server and Windows can work together to provide additional detail and put performance data into an appropriate context. That's what we're going to do now.

1. In the **Performance** utility, select **Counter Logs** if it is not already selected.
2. Right-click **SQL Test** and click **Start**. Wait until the icon turns green before continuing.
3. In the **Profiler Trace Properties** dialog box, click **Run**. You are collecting performance data in both the counter log and in a Profiler trace at the same time.
4. In **SQL Server Management Studio**, execute the following:

```
USE Chapter8
```

5. Clear the query window and type the following:

```
SELECT * INTO SP FROM SALESPERSON
SELECT * INTO CUST FROM CUSTOMER
SELECT * INTO CE FROM CUSTOMEREMPLOYEE
SELECT * INTO PROD FROM PRODUCT
GO
DROP TABLE SP
DROP TABLE CUST
DROP TABLE CE
DROP TABLE PROD
GO
```

6. Execute the statements. When they are finished, execute again, until you have executed all of the statements four times. We are forcing activity in the database.

7. In **SQL Server Profiler**, scroll through and see if you can determine where the statements ran.

8. Open a second query window, type in the following, and execute at least three times:

```
USE Chapter8
GO
SELECT SPNAME, C.SPNUM, CUSTNAME
FROM CUSTOMER C, SALESPERSON SP
WHERE C.SPNUM = SP.SPNUM
SELECT PRODUCTNAME, DESCRIPTION, QUANTITY
FROM SALES, PRODUCT
WHERE SALES.PRODNUM = PRODUCT.PRODNUM
```

9. In **SQL Server Profiler**, open the **File** menu and select **Stop Trace**. In the **Performance** utility, right-click **SQL Test** and select **Stop**.

10. In the **Performance** utility, select **System Monitor**.

11. In the **Performance** utility, click **View Log Data**, shown in Figure 8-17.

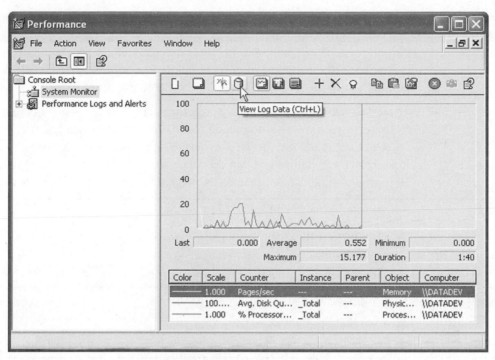

Figure 8-17: View Log Data button

12. Select **Log Files** and click **Add**. Locate and select the file **C:\PerfLogs\SQL Test 000001,** and then click **Open**.

13. On the **Data** page, click **Add** and individually add all available counters not already present. You will get an error message if you try to add a counter that is already there. If you do, click **OK** and continue to the next counter. Only those counters chosen for the log are available. Click **OK**.

14. Position the windows so you can see the **System Monitor** and **Profiler**. This lets you view activity and its result at the same time. Because of the short capture period, the display does not fill the **System Monitor** window. Notice that the Buffer cache usage almost immediately climbs to 100% and stays there. Also, after the first burst, disk activity drops off significantly. That is because read requests, after the initial request for a table, are being serviced from memory instead of the hard disk.

15. Close **SQL Server Management Studio**, **SQL Server Profiler**, the **Performance** utility, and the **Administrative Tools** window. If prompted, do not save changes.

Project 8.4	Recognizing Bottlenecks
Overview	A bottleneck is anything that impairs performance. When discussing bottlenecks, the focus is typically on hardware bottlenecks. The most common culprits are the hard disk, processor, and memory.
	There are two basic options for correcting performance problems resulting from bottlenecks. One is to reduce the load on the server's resources. The other is to upgrade the server's resources so they can stand up to a greater load. However, before you can do either, you need to find the problem. Before you diagnose bottlenecks, you need to be able to recognize them.
Outcomes	After completing this project, you will know how to:
	▲ given operating conditions and symptoms, identify potential bottlenecks
	▲ recommend solutions to bottlenecks
What you'll need	To complete this project, you will need:
	▲ a worksheet below
	▲ an open query window
Completion time	30 minutes
Precautions	Don't worry about the default database at this point.

■ Part A: Case #1

You install SQL Server 2005 on a computer that meets the minimum installation requirements for processor and memory. You have two 30 GB hard disks, so you have more than the minimum hard disk space available. Disk 0 is configured as drives C: and D:, and disk 1 is configured as drives E: and F:. Almost immediately after you deploy the SQL Server database and your database application, users begin complaining about performance. Database files are stored on drives C: and D:, and the database log file is on drive D:. Performance counters tell you that:

- Disk activity on disk 0 is very high.
- There is almost no activity on disk 1.
- Processor use often peaks and holds near 100%.
- The buffer cache hit ratio is less than 50%.
- Memory paging is extremely high.

You move all of the database files and log file to drives E: and F:. Disk activity on disk 1 increases, but activity on disk 0 remains significantly higher than activity on disk 1.

1. What do you suspect as the most likely problem? Why?

    _____

    _____

    _____

2. How would you correct this problem?

    _____

    _____

    _____

3. Why do you think disk 0 activity remains high after moving the database and log files to drive 1?

    _____

    _____

    _____

4. How could you balance this high level between the two hard disks?

    _____

    _____

    _____

5. What, specifically, does the low buffer cache hit ratio tell you?

    _____

    _____

    _____

■ Part B: Case #2

Performance was within acceptable levels when you deployed. Over time, performance has degraded. User activity has increased gradually. The size of the database tables has increased significantly, much faster than expected in the original design specifications. The computer is configured with a standard hard disk (drive C:) and a RAID disk subsystem (drive D:). The operating system and SQL Server 2005 are installed on C:. The database application is deployed individually on the client systems. Database files and the log file are deployed on D:. Disk activity on the RAID disk is within expected parameters. The buffer cache hit ratio exceeds 90%. Processor use is significantly higher than expected. You install a second processor, but it has little impact on application performance.

1. Which hardware component is most likely acting as a performance bottleneck?

_____

_____

_____

2. Performance counters for processor 0 show little change after installing the second processor. Processor 1 shows almost no activity. What is the most likely reason for this?

_____

_____

_____

3. How should you attempt to balance the processor use?

_____

_____

_____

4. Performance does not improve to acceptable levels after correcting the processor problem. Most queries search the entire table. Joins are evaluated using nested loop joins. What is the most likely cause?

_____

_____

_____

5. What, if anything, can you do to correct performance through system hardware?

_____

_____

_____

6. What else can you do to correct the problem?

_____

_____

_____

Project 8.5	Using Indexes and Views
Overview	Indexes sort table data. Clustered indexes physically sort the table in index order. Nonclustered indexes logically organize the data but don't change the table sort order. Having the correct indexes helps increase read query performance. You view execution plans to see index use. Views filter data and provide indirect access to table data. Data can be filtered vertically (by column) or horizontally (by row). SQL Server also supports indexed views, which persist the view to the hard disk, improving disk read performance.
Outcomes	After completing this project, you will know how to: ▲ create indexes ▲ observe index use ▲ create and use views
What you'll need	To complete this project, you will need: ▲ a computer with SQL Server 2005 Evaluation Edition installed ▲ the Chapter8 database
Completion time	30 minutes
Precautions	None

■ Part A: Use indexes

1. Launch **SQL Server Management Studio**, expand **Databases**, right-click **Chapter8**, and select **New Query**.
2. Select **Query** and then **Include Actual Execution Plan**.
3. Execute the following:

```
SELECT * FROM SALESPERSON
```

4. View the execution plan. It should look like Figure 8-18.

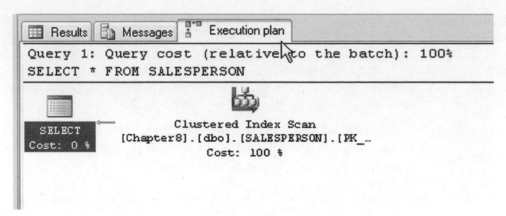

Figure 8-18: Execution plan

The cost represents the relative cost of each step in the execution plan. This query is completed using one index.

5.   Execute the following and review the execution plan.

```
SELECT * FROM SALESPERSON ORDER BY SPNAME
```

6.   Which action shows the highest cost?

_____

_____

7.   Execute the following:

```
CREATE INDEX SNAME
ON SALESPERSON(SPNAME)
```

8.   Execute the following:

```
SELECT * FROM SALESPERSON ORDER BY SPNAME
```

9.   How does the execution plan compare to the one in step 4?

_____

_____

10. Execute the following statements:

```
DROP INDEX SALESPERSON.SNAME
CREATE INDEX SFNAME
ON SALESPERSON(SPFIRSTNAME)
```

11. Execute the queries from steps 4 and 6. How does the execution plan compare?

_____

_____

12. Why doesn't the query use the index SFNAME to resolve the query?

_____

_____

13. Expand **Chapter8** and each of the tables. Review the indexes in each table. Use index properties to view the index key column(s).

14. Assume that several queries join CUSTOMER and SALESPERSON on SPNUM. You want to create an index named SPJOIN to optimize performance. What CREATE INDEX statement would you use to do this?

_____

_____

15. Why would you create the join on that table?

_____

_____

■ Part B: Use views

1. Execute the following:

```
SELECT CUSTNUM, CUSTNAME, SPFIRSTNAME + ' ' +
SPNAME AS [SALESPERSON], HQCITY AS [LOCATION]
FROM CUSTOMER C, SALESPERSON SP
WHERE C.SPNUM = SP.SPNUM
```

2. Review the result.
3. Execute the following:

```
CREATE VIEW AllSPCust AS
SELECT CUSTNUM, CUSTNAME, SPFIRSTNAME + ' ' +
SPNAME AS [SALESPERSON], HQCITY AS [LOCATION]
FROM CUSTOMER C, SALESPERSON SP
WHERE C.SPNUM = SP.SPNUM
```

Tip: You can modify the SELECT statement in the query window instead of retyping everything.

4. Execute the following:

```
SELECT * FROM AllSPCust
```

5. How does the result compare to the result in step 1?

    _____

    _____

6. Create a view named v_Cust_137 that returns the same information for customers assigned to salesperson 137. What query should you use?

    _____

    _____

7. Execute the query and test the view. How many rows does it return?

    _____

    _____

8. For what salesperson?

    _____

    _____

9. Create a view named v_Cust_361 that returns the same information for salesperson 361. What command do you use?

    _____

    _____

10. Which salesperson does the view return?

_____

_____

11. You want to create a view named PhoneList that returns last name, first name, SPNUM, and extension in name order. How can you test the view before creating it?

_____

_____

12. Create the view. What columns, if any, must be qualified with the table name?

_____

_____

Project 8.6	Using Procedures and Functions
Overview	Procedures and functions provide another way to isolate the user from database tables and to ensure that operations are performed consistently. Typically, you will use a function when you need a scalar value or table result returned. The main advantage is that the functions you create can be used like system functions, including as a data source in queries.
Outcomes	After completing this project, you will know how to: ▲ create and test a procedure ▲ create and test views
What you'll need	To complete this project, you will need: ▲ a computer with SQL Server 2005 Evaluation Edition installed ▲ the Chapter8 database
Completion time	30 minutes
Precautions	None

■ Part A: Create procedures

Parameters are optional for procedures. You can include input and output parameters, as appropriate, in the procedure definition.

1. Launch **SQL Server Management Studio**, expand **Databases**, right-click **Chapter8**, and select **New Query**.

2. Execute the following:

```
CREATE PROC p_AddOffice
@OFFNUM CHAR(4), @EXTENSION CHAR(4), @SIZE INT = 120
AS
INSERT OFFICE VALUES (@OFFNUM, @EXTENSION, @SIZE)
```

3. How many parameters does the procedure have?

_____

4. Execute the following to test:

```
p_ADDOFFICE '3000', '4443', 200
GO
p_ADDOFFICE '3001', '4442'
```

5. Why can you use only two parameters in the second example?

_____

_____

6. Retrieve all rows from OFFICE to verify that the procedure worked. What is the size value for office 3001?

_____

_____

7. Create the following procedure:

```
CREATE PROC p_Count
@count int OUTPUT
AS
set @count = (select count(*) from customer)
RETURN @count
```

Notice that you can, in most cases, use either upper- or lowercase characters. Uppercase is often used for commands in documentation to make them stand out, but it isn't required.

8. Write a batch to retrieve the value. Enter your batch below. Test to ensure that it works. **Tip:** Use PRINT @varname to view the result.

_____

_____

_____

9. Using the procedure in step 4 as your model, create a procedure named CountBySP to return a count by SPNUM.

10. What changes must you make?

_____

_____

11. Test your procedure to verify that it works.

■ Part B: Create functions

Functions always return a value. Input parameters are optional.

1. Create the following function:

```
CREATE FUNCTION f_count
()
RETURNS INT
BEGIN
DECLARE @CT AS INT
SET @CT = (SELECT COUNT(*) FROM CUSTOMER)
RETURN @CT
END
```

2. Execute the following to test:

```
select dbo.f_count()
```

3. What is the return value?

_____

4. What kind of function did you create?

   _____

5. Create a function that returns a table, using the following:

```
CREATE FUNCTION fn_SPCUST
()
RETURNS TABLE
AS
RETURN (SELECT CUSTNUM, CUSTNAME, SPFIRSTNAME + ' ' +
SPNAME AS [SALESPERSON], HQCITY AS [LOCATION]
FROM CUSTOMER C, SALESPERSON SP
WHERE C.SPNUM = SP.SPNUM)
```

6. What would you run to test this function? (**Tip:** Include the schema, dbo, in the function name.)

   _____

   _____

7. Test the function.
8. Using the function in step 5 as your guide, create a table-valued function that accepts a salesperson number (as CHAR(3)) and returns the same information, but for that salesperson only. Name the function f_bySP.
9. What should you use?

   _____

10. Test the function.

9
DATABASE ADMINISTRATION

PROJECTS

Project 9.1	Understanding Administration
Overview	As with any other aspect of working with data and databases, it's important to understand terms and concepts related to administration. It's also important to understand typical responsibilities and how they are usually delegated as administrative tasks.
Outcomes	After completing this project, you will know how to: ▲ explain terms related to data administration monitoring ▲ explain terms related to database administration
What you'll need	To complete this project, you will need: ▲ the worksheet below
Completion time	20 minutes
Precautions	None

The worksheet below includes a list of terms on the left and descriptions on the right. Match each term with the description that it most closely matches. You will use all descriptions. Each description can be used only once.

____ Data administrator

A. Recorded activity, such as user activity or resource use tracked through performance monitoring

____ Database administrator

B. Requirements regarding naming, value use, and allowable value types and ranges

____ System analyst

C. Person, application, or department using data

____ Maintenance plan

D. Individual who analyzes complex systems and their interactions to determine how to use computers to meet business requirements

____ Log

E. Action that does not require operator intervention

____ Audit trail

F. Action that requires operator intervention

____ Business problem

G. Means of monitoring when a performance threshold is reached or exceeded

____ Arbitration

H. Individual with operationally oriented responsibilities

___ Manual task

I. Decision point within a maintenance plan used to control execution

___ Automated task

J. Anything that adversely affects performance

___ Data standards

K. Act of resolving disputes between parties in disagreement

___ Precedence constraint

L. Set of defined management tasks executing on a periodic schedule

___ Data flow

M. Anything that prevents a business from operating as it should

___ Consumer

N. Ongoing record of user access and activity

___ Bottleneck

O. Path taken by data from its producer or owner to its consumer

___ Alert

P. Individual with responsibilities related to planning and analysis

Project 9.2	Understanding Roles and Responsibilities
Overview	Even though the lines often become blurred, it's important to have, as a starting point, an understanding of the data and database administration roles and responsibilities. When presented with an administration requirement, you should be able to determine who has primary responsibility, keeping in mind that responsibilities do overlap. Even if one role has primary responsibility for a task, the other is often expected to consult or assist. Some responsibilities are related in that each role has a different specific task expectation, but both are required to meet the responsibility. Although the data administrator is usually responsible for determining what needs to be done in these cases, the job of meeting that need falls on the database administrator.
Outcomes	After completing this project, you will know how to: ▲ identify data administrator responsibilities ▲ identify database administrator responsibilities
What you'll need	To complete this project, you will need: ▲ the worksheet below
Completion time	30 minutes
Precautions	None

For each task description or requirement in Table 9-1, enter "Data" if it is a data administration responsibility or "Database" if it is a database administration responsibility. In each case, even when the responsibilities overlap, one role will have the primary responsibility.

Table 9-1: Task statements and responsibilities

Statement	Responsibility
As we qualify new vendors, we need to identify the data format requirements for generating EDI purchase orders.	
The individual salesperson's customer records have been integrated into the master database. No one wants to share the data with anyone else. We need them to share data, but we want to keep problems with attitudes and egos to a minimum.	
Look, someone has to create the tables.	
We'll start with point of sale and work our way back. Other than the products and customers, what entities are involved?	
They've added a second RAID disk subsystem to the database server. We need to split the data between the two disk subsystems.	

Statement	Responsibility
All users must be prevented from adding tables to the database. In fact, we also don't want them making changes to the existing tables.	
From now on, if an inventory item has a substitution available, we need to track that along with the inventory item. That means adding another column to the Inventory table. Make sure it allows NULL values.	
We've integrated the data from the company we acquired. Someone needs to prepare an executive summary explaining what's there. Today!	
Make sure that the associates working point of sale can't see anything in the Product table except the item SKU, description, quantity on hand, and selling price.	
Each local office needs to track their inventory locally. We'll keep a master copy here in the home office. Any time one of the local copies is updated, we need to make sure that the master copy is updated at the same time. Set it up so the change is backed out if there's any kind of problem with either update.	
Those stores we bought have 5 years worth of data in Access databases. Right now, it's just sitting around. How can we integrate it with our SQL Server database?	
By how much can we expect data storage needs to grow over the next 2 years?	
In the morning, finishing a customer order takes 30 seconds at most and I have the entry screen back. After 3:00 PM, it takes more than 2 minutes. I keep wondering if my computer locked up.	
We have all of this customer sales history and nobody is using it. Someone needs to make sure that marketing knows about it.	
I'm trying to start an order, but I keep getting an error message – something about it not finding the server.	
I'm not sure, but I think I smelled smoke coming from the server room. You know, that scorched electronics smell? I just thought you'd want to know about it.	
Make sure that table column names in the new database make sense. Those alphanumeric things we have now are useless. For what you're getting paid, you should be able to figure out a better way.	
Next step, normalization. Excited yet?	

Statement	Responsibility
The application will access tables through views. That's in the design spec. Here's a list of views that the programmers will need, including the tables and columns. Make it happen.	
Someone is making changes to customer accounting records. I know because our accounts are completely out of balance. I get an error every time I try to run a summary and it won't go any further. First, stop it. Second, find out who. Third, make sure it doesn't happen again. Ever. Next time, it's your job on the line.	
Run a full backup over the weekend. Run transaction log backups twice a day. I want these running automatically, regardless of whether there's anyone around.	

Project 9.3	Matching Life Cycle Requirements
Overview	One way of looking at a database application project is through the project life cycle. You can describe the life cycle as having four phases: design, implementation, production, and retirement. Each phase has administration responsibilities and task requirements for both data administration and database administration. You should be able to identify the responsibilities linked to each of these phases, as well as the responsible role.
Outcomes	After completing this project, you will know how to: ▲ identify responsibilities by life cycle phase
What you'll need	To complete this project, you will need: ▲ the worksheet below
Completion time	60 minutes
Precautions	None

Below is a table with four columns for the four life cycle phases and a list of responsibilities. For each responsibility, add it to the appropriate column. A single responsibility can be listed in multiple columns. Each responsibility will be added to at least one column. Each column will have at least one responsibility when completed.

The responsibilities list is not meant to be a complete list of all possible responsibilities. Instead, it is representative of some of the most common responsibilities. Responsibilities can be listed in any order.

Table 9-2: Database life cycle

Design	Implementation	Production	Retirement

Responsibilities

Historic archives

Backups

Monitor performance

Create tables

Create views

Normalization

Performance tuning

Identify entities

Pick data types

Initial testing

Data file placement

New user access

New user permissions

Plan data migration

Baseline performance collection

Data entry

Physical data migration

Naming standards

Access standards

Integrating external data

Day-to-day maintenance

Relationships

Identify external data

Deploy database

Table defragmentation

User interviews

Patches and service packs

DBMS version upgrades

Project 9.4	Resolving Administration Issues
Overview	Administrators must be able to review the current situation to identify outstanding issues and to efficiently resolve those issues. While resolving one issue, it's not unusual to discover another issue that is either related or was being masked by the first issue.
	Administration needs to include both one-time or as-needed activities and periodic activities that must be performed on a regular schedule. How you resolve a specific issue, either with an as-needed solution or with a periodic scheduled solution, depends on the task requirements.
Outcomes	After completing this project, you will know how to: ▲ identify administration issues ▲ recommend steps to resolve administration issues
What you'll need	To complete this project, you will need: ▲ the worksheet below
Completion time	60 minutes
Precautions	None

Below, you are presented with two short case studies. The cases studies include simulated user and manager interviews. These interviews indicate various possible problems. Read the case studies and answer the questions that follow.

■ Part A: Case Study #1

You've been hired to replace the current database administrator. There is only a 2-day overlap between you arriving and the current administrator leaving. The outgoing administrator has offered to give you what help he can during those 2 days. You haven't met the data administrator yet, but you've been told that she designed the current database and takes change recommendations personally.

Outgoing Database Administrator

We're having performance problems, but they're intermittent and creep in over time. It's due to fragmentation caused by data changes in the tables that have the customer order, purchase order, and accounting data. Index rebuilds fix the problem, but they take forever and interrupt operations. The business runs 24/7, so there are few times when we run the rebuilds. If we ran them more often, they might run faster.

Information Services (IS) Manager

All of our worldwide operations rely on data stored on our servers in New York. We have a distributed data environment, but all of the servers are in the same geographic location. Each server is configured as a server cluster with two computers sharing one external data store. Once reason for this is that it lets us have one server running while we do planned maintenance on the other. If one server goes down, the other takes over for it automatically. However, we're not using redundant storage, so backups are critical. We can't afford to have to repost more than 1 hour's worth of data.

The data include tables partitioned across different server clusters. Our applications take care of keeping data updates consistent between the servers, but if you ever make changes to database object structure, you need to make sure it's done to all affected servers at the same time.

Human Resources

Personnel changes are rather regular. At least one person gets hired or fired every week, usually more. Our standard is that when a user is called in for termination, access to all company data is cut off immediately. We call IS about the status change when we call the employee. When a new hire starts, their data access should be ready to go the first time they log on to the network.

Purchasing

EDI is a big part of our operations. Nearly all of our vendors and customers use EDI order management systems. We have one programmer who sets things up whenever we get a new vendor or customer, but it takes too long and, according to the programmer, it's too complicated. Data have to be pulled from several sources. It would be better if it came from a single source.

1. What actions should the data administrator take to resolve purchasing needs?

   _____

   _____

   _____

2. What actions should the database administrator take to resolve purchasing needs?

   _____

   _____

   _____

3. Should changes that affect table structure on partitioned tables be run as manual or automated procedures? Why?

   _____

   _____

   _____

4. How can you minimize the impact of index fragmentation and avoid the need for manual intervention? The solution should have minimal impact on normal operations.

   _____

   _____

   _____

5. What is the maximum time between backups? Why?

   _____

   _____

   _____

6. Should backups be manual or automated? Explain your answer.

   _____

   _____

   _____

7. Should the actions taken when an employee is fired be run as manual or automated procedures? Explain your answer.

   _____

   _____

   _____

8. If given advance warning of a day or more, how could actions related to new hire employees be automated?

   _____

   _____

   _____

9. Other than Purchasing, which interviews (if any) have identified data administration needs?

_____

_____

_____

10. Would remote data communications be a critical concern in this environment? Why or why not?

_____

_____

_____

■ Part B: Case Study #2

You are a consultant specializing in data and database administration. You are meeting with various people who work for a potential new client. Before taking them on as a client, you want to get some idea of what they need and how much work it's going to take.

Owner

We're not exactly a small business, but we're not all that big. We don't have any programmers, exactly, but we have some people who know Visual Basic and take care of some small applications we've written ourselves. If we need something big or something they don't know how to do, we contract out. There's a lot of stuff we just do from query windows because it's easier. At least, it's faster. My biggest concern is about what things they might see that they shouldn't.

Accountant

Accounting is separate from the business production database. I pull the information that I need off the business database and then manually post it in the accounting application. It would be better if I could get things set up where I just get the information I need. Last time we had someone in, he created some views that give me the data, but they don't limit it by date, so it's still more complicated than I like. He even showed me how to create them and I guess I could do it that way, but it seems like more work than it's really worth. Eventually, we want to automate the whole process.

Data Entry Lead

We have an application for entering information about equipment and services, but not new customers. I have a checklist cheatsheet, but it's easy to mistype something and murder to find the mistake. It's crazy to have to type all that. Most of the time it's the same for every customer. Sure, there are exceptions, but not that many.

"Computer Guy"

If something goes wrong with one of the computers, it's my job to fix it. I'm self-taught mostly. If it wasn't for my library and the Internet, I'd be lost most of the time. The one thing I don't do is any of the Visual Basic stuff. Don't know how, don't want to know how. I can do some of the database stuff if I have to. I don't mind the regular maintenance stuff, but it does get time consuming and I'm doing the same thing every month.

What I don't like is going in and making changes, and I get nervous if there's a problem with the database because most of the time I have no idea how to fix it. My biggest problem is that the stupid thing keeps growing, and I'm not sure why because it doesn't need the space. Must be something in the application. About every other month, I have to run through my checklist to shrink down the database file. If I don't catch it in time, we run out of space and things really go crazy. I wish there was some way I could get a warning when it gets close. Or better yet, have the stupid thing fix itself.

1. How can you relieve the owner's biggest concern?

    _____

    _____

    _____

2. How can you correct the database size problem? The solution should be automatic and should run as needed.

    _____

    _____

    _____

3. How can you fully automate the solution so available space never reaches a threshold point?

    _____

    _____

    _____

4. Most of the queries that directly access database tables retrieve data based on a small number of variable parameters. What could you create to improve security while meeting specific data needs?

    _____

    _____

    _____

5. What kind of database object could you use to make data entry easier? Explain your answer.

_____

_____

_____

6. With what should you replace the views currently being used by the accountant? Explain your answer.

_____

_____

_____

7. How can you make regular maintenance easier for the "computer guy?"

_____

_____

_____

8. How can you let the "computer guy" know if there is a problem?

_____

_____

_____

Project 9.5	Managing "As-Needed" and Periodic Tasks
Overview	Many administrative tasks are common to all, or nearly all, databases. Even so, there can be differences in the specifics of how they are run or in execution schedules.
	There are different ways of looking at task requirements. One is when the tasks are run. In this context, you can divide tasks into "as-needed" and periodic tasks. As-needed tasks are just what the name implies, tasks that you run only as necessary. This can include things like adding database objects (tables, views, logins, users), responding to database conditions, or correcting errors. Periodic tasks are those that are part of regular, ongoing maintenance, such as checking database consistency and running backups.
	Even though the details of how you perform the tasks vary by DBMS, it's good to get some exposure to actual administrative tasks. There are usually enough similarities that what you learn about one DBMS can be applied to another. This includes working with periodic tasks, such as the steps involved in creating a SQL Server Maintenance Plan.
Outcomes	After completing this project, you will know how to: ▲ perform as-needed administrative tasks ▲ schedule tasks for execution ▲ create a maintenance plan
What you'll need	To complete this project, you will need: ▲ a computer with SQL Server 2005 Evaluation Edition installed ▲ the AdventureWorks database
Completion time	60 minutes
Precautions	Limit your changes to those specifically called out in this project. Do not make changes to any databases other than AdventureWorks.

■ Part A: Schedule baseline collection

Baseline performance statistic collection is an "as-needed" activity. It is done after you first implement the database. You might want to collect new baseline data after upgrading server hardware or software or after major revisions to your database application. You can use the Performance utility to collect the data unattended.

1. Open the **Control Panel** and launch **Administrative Tools**.
2. Double-click **Performance**.
3. Expand **Performance Logs and Alerts**.
4. Right-click **Counter Logs** and select **New Log Settings**.

5. Name the log **MorningBase** and click **OK**.

6. Add the counters listed in Table 9-3. Click **Explain** if you want to learn more about individual counters. Click **Close** when finished adding counters.

Table 9-3: Log counters

Performance Object	Performance Counter	Instance
Processor	% Processor Time	Total
Processor	% User Time	Total
Memory	Pages/sec	N/A
Memory	Page Faults/sec	N/A
Memory	Available MBytes	N/A
PhysicalDisk	Avg. Disk Queue Length	Add a counter for each physical disk instance
PhysicalDisk	Disk Bytes/sec	Add a counter for each physical disk instance

7. Leave the remaining options at default. Your settings should look similar to Figure 9-1.

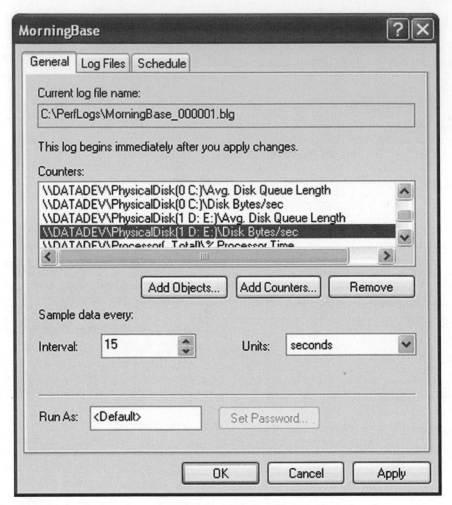

Figure 9-1: Log counters

8. Select the **Log Files** tab.

9. Choose **Text File (Comma delimited)** as the log file type.

10. Click **Configure.**

11. Enter the file path as **C:\BaseLogs**.

12. Click **OK**. Click **Yes** when prompted to create the folder. Your settings should look like Figure 9-2.

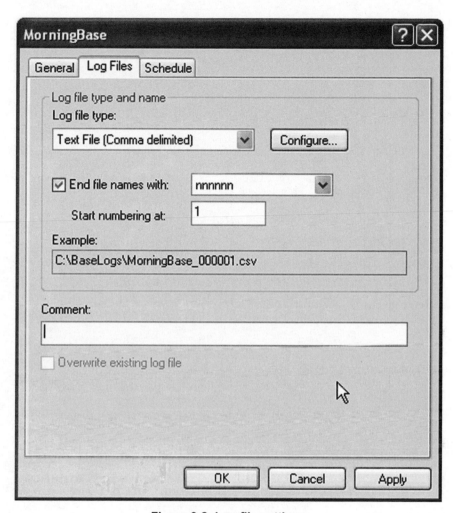

Figure 9-2: Log file settings

13. Select the **Schedule** tab.

14. Configure the log to start at 9:00 AM tomorrow and end at 10:00 AM tomorrow. Your settings will look similar to Figure 9-3.

Figure 9-3: Schedule settings

15. Click **OK** to create the log.

16. Create a second log file. For this file, name the file **AfternoonLog**, save the log to the same folder, configure the log to start at 2:00 PM tomorrow and end at 3:30 PM tomorrow, and save the settings and create the **Counter Log.**

17. Select **Counter Logs**. The logs you created should be listed as shown in Figure 9-4.

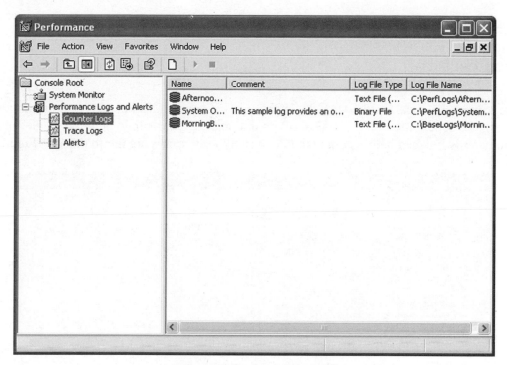

Figure 9-4: New counter logs

18. Exit the **Performance** utility. The logs will run and collect data as scheduled.

■ Part B: Check database consistency

You can use the database consistency checker (DBCC) utility to check database consistency. DBCC supports several commands for this purpose, letting you check the database as a whole or check individual database tables for problems such as physical data page errors or table fragmentation. Other DBCC commands let you collect performance and database usage information. You can even use DBCC to shrink a database or database files.

We're going to use DBCC CHECKDB. This command runs a general check and validation of the database. It checks physical storage for errors, individually checks and validates each database table, and checks the contents of any indexed views that database contains.

DBCC is specific to Microsoft's Transact-SQL language set. It is not part of the standard SQL language. DBCC runs from a query prompt.

1. Launch **SQL Server Management Studio**, expand **Databases**, and expand **AdventureWorks**.

2. Right-click **AdventureWorks** and select **New Query**. Verify that **AdventureWorks** is selected as the default database.

3. Execute the following:

```
DBCC CHECKDB
```

4. The command runs on the default database. The command can take several minutes to complete, depending on the speed of your computer and other activity. Wait until the command is finished before continuing. You should see results similar to those in Figure 9-5.

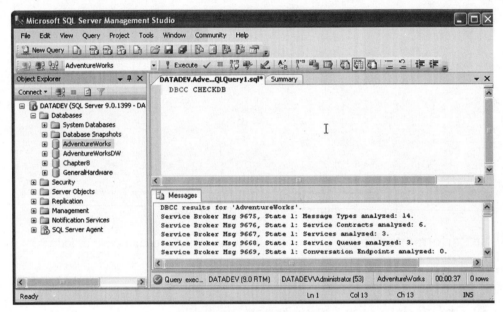

Figure 9-5: DBCC results

5. Scroll through the results. What information is returned about each of the database tables?

_____

_____

_____

6. Scroll to the end of the results. What kind of errors are mentioned?

_____

_____

_____

7. How many errors were found?

_____

_____

_____

8. Do not exit **SQL Server Management Studio**.

■ Part C: Create a maintenance plan

You will use the Maintenance Plan Wizard to create a Maintenance Plan for AdventureWorks. When finished, you will verify that the plan was created and change the execution schedule. Part of your maintenance plan will include checking database consistency and shrinking the database, effectively automating procedures you can run manually with the DBCC command.

1. In **SQL Server Management Studio Object Explorer**, expand **Management**.
2. Right-click **Maintenance Plans** and **Maintenance Plan Wizard**.
3. Click **Next**.
4. Name the plan **Monthly Maintenance**. Leave the target server and connection information at default. Click **Next**.
5. Select the following tasks:

    *   Check Database Integrity
    *   Shrink Database
    *   Rebuild Index
    *   Back Up Database (Full)

6. Click **Next.**
7. Select **Back Up Database (Full)** and click **Move Up** until it is at the top of the list, as shown in Figure 9-6.

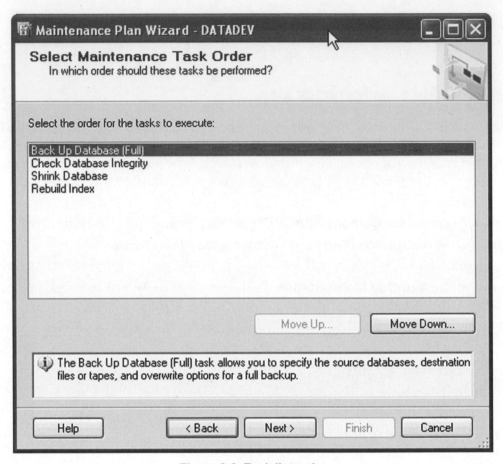

Figure 9-6: Task list order

8. Click **Next**.

9. Click the drop-down arrow for databases, choose **AdventureWorks**, and click **OK**.

10. At the bottom of the page, select **Verify backup integrity**. The page should look like Figure 9-7.

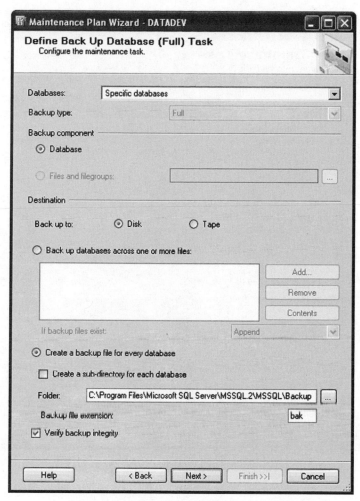

Figure 9-7: Back Up Database (Full) Task

11. Click **Next**.

12. On the **Define Check Database Integrity Task** page, choose **AdventureWorks** as on the previous page, and then click **Next** to continue.

13. On the **Define Shrink Database Task** page, choose **AdventureWorks**, set the size at which to shrink the database to **10** MB, and return the space to the operating system. The page should look like Figure 9-8.

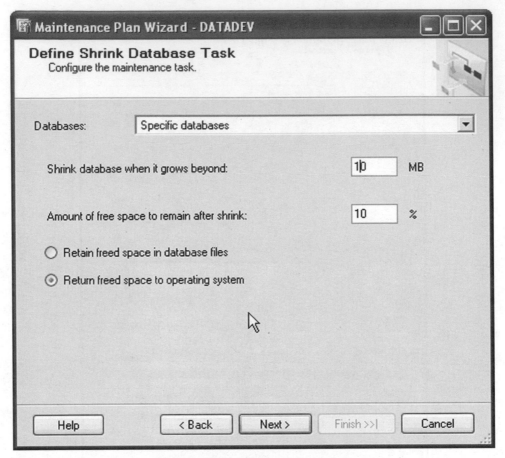

Figure 9-8: Shrink Database Task

14. Click **Next**.

15. On the **Define Rebuild Index Task** page, choose **Adventure Works**, choose the object type **Tables and Views**, change free space percentage to **30%**, and select all **Advanced options**.

16. Your completed page should look like Figure 9-9.

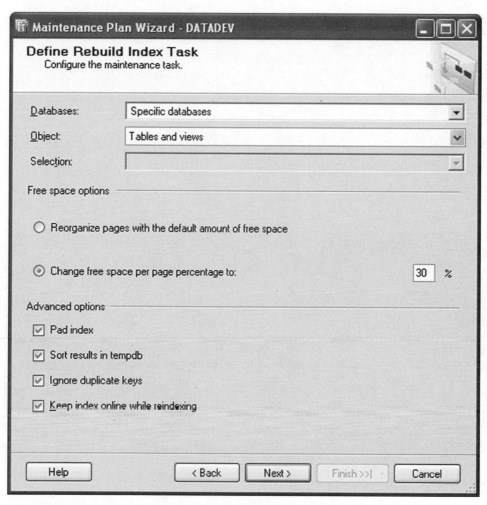

Figure 9-9: Rebuild Index Task

17. Click **Next**.

18. On the **Schedule Plan Properties** page, click **Change**.

19. Name the schedule **StndMonthly**.

20. Set the frequency as **Monthly** on the first Sunday of each month at 12:00 AM. Leave the other settings at default. Your schedule should be similar to Figure 9-10.

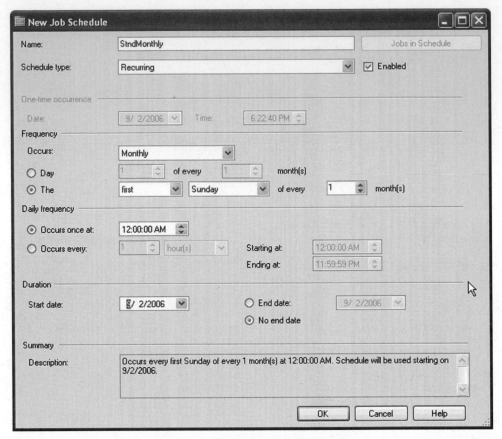

Figure 9-10: Execution schedule

21. What is entered as the default start date?

_____

22. What is the default end date?

_____

23. Click **OK**.
24. Click **Next**.
25. Leave the reporting options at default and click **Next**.
26. Review the plan actions and click **Finish**.
27. SQL Server will create the maintenance plan. Click **Close** when the dialog box reports that it is finished.
28. Expand **Maintenance Plans**. Verify that your plan is listed.
29. Exit **SQL Server Management Studio**.

10
TRANSACTIONS AND LOCKING

PROJECTS

Project 10.1	Understanding Transactions and Locking
Overview	Transaction processing is a major part of most database applications. Because of this, it is important that you understand the terminology associated with transactions and locking technologies that are used to help ensure consistency and minimize concurrency errors. Keep in mind that the terms presented here are presented in the context of transactions, transaction isolation, and locking. Some terms, used in a different context, can have a different meaning.
Outcomes	After completing this project, you will know how to: ▲ explain key terms related to transaction processing ▲ explain key terms related to transaction isolation and locking
What you'll need	To complete this project, you will need: ▲ the worksheet below
Completion time	20 minutes
Precautions	None

The worksheet below a list of terms on the left and descriptions on the right. Match each term with the description that it most closely matches. You will use all descriptions. Each description can be used only once.

___ Deadlock

A. Condition where data changes between subsequent reads of the same data by a transaction

___ Dirty page

B. Referring to the fact that all statements must execute as a group or none of the statements execute

___ Atomicity

C. Transaction isolation level that prevents reading uncommitted data or other transactions changing data read by the transaction

___ Lock

D. Transaction type in which the entire transaction is controlled through statements to initiate and complete the transaction

___ Read committed

E. Most restrictive transaction isolation level

___ Repeatable read

F. Process of backing out changes made by an unsuccessful transaction

	Nonrepeatable read	G. Cache memory that has been updated, but the update has not been written to the hard disk
	Phantom	H. Process of successfully completing a transaction and finalizing its changes
	Serializable	I. Set of statements that must either complete as a group or have the changes backed out as a group
	Commit	J. Transaction type in which the transaction initiates automatically, but must be completed manually
	Rollback	K. Temporary restriction placed on a database object, preventing access to the object by statements outside the transaction that hold the lock
	Transaction	L. Ensuring that one transaction does not interfere with another transaction
	Isolation	M. Data row that appears or disappears during a subsequent read of a data range
	Explicit	N. Condition in which two transactions block each others' access to data resources
	Implicit	O. Transaction isolation level that prevents dirty reads, but does not prevent nonrepeatable reads or phantoms

Project 10.2	Understanding Transaction Types
Overview	There are several ways in which you can categorize transactions. One is identifying them as implicit or explicit transactions. Many DBMSs, as well as most data APIs, provide support for both transaction types, but they are not interchangeable. It's important that you recognize features of each and when it is appropriate to use each type.
Outcomes	After completing this project, you will know how to: ▲ recognize features of implicit transactions ▲ recognize features of explicit transactions
What you'll need	To complete this project, you will need: ▲ the worksheet below ▲ the sample data files (Chapter10.mdf and Chapter10.ldf) ▲ a computer running SQL Server 2005
Completion time	45 minutes
Precautions	Create a folder named Chap10Data at the root of drive C: and copy the sample database files to that folder before starting this activity. You should be logged in as an administrator at the beginning of the activity steps. Do not make changes to any database other than Chapter10. This project is a prerequisite for most of the remaining activities in this chapter.

■ Part A: Identify transaction types

For each statement in the left column of Table 10-1, identify whether the statement applies to implicit transactions, explicit transactions, both, or neither.

Table 10-1: Transaction descriptions

Description	Type
Transaction must be initiated by running BEGIN TRAN.	
Transaction starts automatically after the previous transaction completes.	
Each statement is treated as an independent transaction.	
Transaction must be completed by running either COMMIT TRAN or ROLLBACK TRAN.	
Default transaction type configuration for SQL Server 2005.	

Description	Type
Typically used only when needed to support legacy applications that expect this transaction type.	
All transaction statements must commit or rollback as a group.	
If pending when the connection in which it was executed is closed, the transaction is rolled back.	
After a server shuts down suddenly and is restarted, pending transactions in the transaction log are committed during recovery.	
Supported by ADO.NET API.	
Supported by ODBC.	
Can run concurrently with other transactions.	

■ Part B: Use transaction types

1. Open the **Start** menu, point to **All Programs**, point to **Microsoft SQL Server 2005**, and then select **SQL Server Management Studio**.
2. If necessary, expand the local server. Right-click **Databases** and select **Attach**.
3. Click **Add**.
4. Locate and select **C:\Chap10Data\Chapter10.mdf** and click **OK**.
5. In the **Attach Databases** dialog box, click **OK** to attach the database.
6. Expand **Databases**. If **Chapter10** is not listed, right-click **Databases** and select **Refresh**.
7. Open the **Help** menu and select **Index**.
8. In the **Look for:** box, type **implicit_transactions**.
9. Click the **IMPLICIT_TRANSACTIONS** option. Review the statements that will begin an implicit transaction. Close the **Help** window when finished.

■ Part C: Test transaction type features

1. Right-click **Chapter10** and select **New query**.
2. Execute the following:

```
CREATE TABLE TranTest
(C1 int, C2 varchar(20))
```

3. Execute the following to count the number of open transactions:

```
SELECT @@TRANCOUNT
```

4. What is the result?

    _____

5. What does this tell you about implicit transactions?

    _____

    _____

    _____

6. What is the default transaction type, and how does it affect statement processing?

    _____

    _____

    _____

    _____

7. Drop the table created in step 2.

8. Using the help information viewed earlier, use the **SET** command to enable implicit transactions. What statement will you run?

    _____

    _____

    _____

9. Execute the following:

```
RECONFIGURE
GO
CREATE TABLE TranTest
(C1 int, C2 varchar(20))
```

10. Count the number of open transactions. What value is returned?

    _____

    _____

11. In **Object Explorer**, expand **Chapter10**, and then click the **expand (+)** sign for **Tables**. What happens?

    _____

    _____

12. Commit the transaction. Right-click **Tables**, select **Refresh**, and then expand **Tables**. Do you see the table **TranTest** listed?

    _____

    _____

13. Execute the following statements:

    ```
    select * into spcopy from salesperson
    select * from spcopy
    ```

14. How many open transactions does the connection currently have?

    _____

    _____

15. Execute the following:

    ```
    CREATE TABLE TranTest2
    (C1 int, C2 varchar(20))
    ```

16. What is the transaction count?

    _____

    _____

17. Why hasn't the count increased?

    _____

    _____

18. Rollback the transaction.
19. Execute the following:

    ```
    select * from spcopy
    ```

20. What happens?

    _____

    _____

21. Explain why the statement ran in step 13, but not now.

    _____

    _____

22. Right-click **Tables** and select **Refresh**. Do you see the table **spcopy** or **TranTest2** listed?

    _____

    _____

23. Disable implicit transactions. What statement will you run?

    _____

    _____

24. Execute the following:

    ```
    RECONFIGURE
    GO
    CREATE TABLE TranTest2
    (C1 int, C2 varchar(20))
    ```

25. What is the transaction count?

    _____

    _____

26. Verify that the table is listed, and then drop the **TranTest2** table.
27. Execute the following:

    ```
    BEGIN TRAN
    CREATE TABLE TranTest2
    (C1 int, C2 varchar(20))
    ```

28. What is the transaction count?

    _____

    _____

29. Commit the transaction and verify that the table is listed in the **Tables** folder.
30. Execute the following:

```
begin tran
select * into spcopy from salesperson
select * from spcopy
```

31. What is the transaction count?

_____

_____

32. Execute the following:

```
BEGIN TRAN
CREATE TABLE TranTest3
(C1 int, C2 varchar(20))
```

33. What is the transaction count?

_____

_____

34. Execute the following:

```
COMMIT TRAN
```

35. What is the new transaction count? Why?

_____

_____

36. What, if anything, would you do to write all changes to disk?

_____

_____

37. Write all changes to disk.

38. Execute the following:

```
BEGIN TRAN
CREATE TABLE NestTranTest1
(C1 int, C2 varchar(20))
BEGIN TRAN
CREATE TABLE NestTranTest2
(C1 int, C2 varchar(20))
```

39. What is the transaction count?

_____

_____

40. Execute the following:

```
ROLLBACK TRAN
```

41. What is the transaction count? Why?

_____

_____

42. Close the query window. Do not save changes when prompted.
43. Exit **SQL Server Management Studio**.

Project 10.3	Understanding Transaction Isolation and Locking
Overview	Transaction isolation settings determine the impact transactions can potentially have on each other. They help determine the types of locks acquired by transactions. It's important to understand the impact of transaction isolation levels and locks on transaction processing. This will help you in selecting the proper level when using transactions.
	The higher the transaction isolation level, the less likely the transaction is to be affected by other transactions, and the less likely that concurrency errors might occur. However, higher isolation levels mean that errors related to blocked transactions become more likely.
Outcomes	After completing this project, you will know how to:
	▲ identify features of transaction isolation levels
	▲ set and test transaction isolation levels
What you'll need	To complete this project, you will need:
	▲ the worksheet below
	▲ a computer running SQL Server 2005 with the Chapter10 sample database attached
Completion time	60 minutes
Precautions	You should be logged in as an administrator at the beginning of the project. Do not make changes to any database other than Chapter10.
	Watch carefully while running commands to make sure that you are executing the statements in the correct query window.

■ Part A: Define transaction isolation levels

The column on the left has a list of standard transaction isolation levels as defined by the SQL-99 standard. The column on the right is a list of potential concurrency errors. In Table 10-2, under "Isolation Level", list the transaction isolation levels from least restrictive to most restrictive. Under "Protects Against" and "Doesn't Protect Against", list the concurrency errors, as appropriate.

Transaction Isolation Levels

Read committed

Repeatable read

Serializable

Read uncommitted

Concurrency errors

Dirty read

Nonrepeatable read

Phantom read

Table 10-2: Transaction Isolation levels

Isolation Level	Protects Against	Doesn't Protect Against

■ **Part B: Use transaction isolation levels**

1. Launch **SQL Server Management Studio**.
2. Expand **Databases**.
3. Right-click **Chapter10** and select **New Query**. This will be referred to as **Query1** throughout this activity.
4. Right-click **Chapter 10** and select **New Query**. This will be referred to as **Query2** throughout this activity. **Tip:** The Windows menu lets you switch between query windows.

5. What is the default transaction isolation level? **Tip:** Look up transaction isolation in the online help if you aren't sure.

_____

_____

6. In **Query1**, execute the following:

```
BEGIN TRAN
SELECT * FROM EmpCount
INSERT EmpCount VALUES ('2002', 57)
SELECT * FROM EmpCount
```

7. What happens?

_____

_____

8. In **Query2**, execute the following:

```
INSERT EmpCount VALUES ('2003', 66)
```

9. What happens?

_____

_____

10. In **Query1**, execute the following:

```
SELECT * FROM EmpCount
```

11. How is the result different than step 6?

_____

_____

12. This is an example of what kind of concurrency error, if any?

_____

_____

13. Should you expect the error to be prevented by the default transaction isolation type?

_____

_____

14. In **Query2**, execute the following:

```
UPDATE EmpCount SET COUNT = 6 WHERE Customer = '2198'
```

15. What happens?

_____

_____

16. In **Query1**, execute the following:

```
COMMIT TRAN
```

17. What happens in **Query2?**

_____

_____

18. What about the default isolation level prevented the command from executing before you completed the transaction in **Query1**?

_____

_____

■ **Part C: Test serializable isolation**

1. In **Query1**, execute the following:

```
SET TRANSACTION ISOLATION LEVEL SERIALIZABLE
RECONFIGURE
```

2. What is the current transaction isolation level in **Query1**? Explain your answer.

_____

_____

3. What is the current transaction isolation level in **Query2**? Explain your answer.

_____

_____

4. In **Query1**, execute the following:

```
BEGIN TRAN
INSERT EmpCount VALUES ('2004', 57)
SELECT * FROM EmpCount
```

5. In **Query2**, execute the following:

```
UPDATE EmpCount SET COUNT = 7 WHERE Customer = '2198'
```

6. What happens?

_____

_____

7. Rollback the transaction in **Query1**, and verify that the transaction in **Query2** completes and that the change was made. What can you run in **Query2** to verify this?

_____

_____

8. In **Query1**, execute the following:

```
BEGIN TRAN
INSERT EmpCount VALUES ('2004', 57)
SELECT * FROM EmpCount
```

9. In **Query2**, execute the following:

```
INSERT EmpCount VALUES ('2005', 66)
```

10. What happens and why?

_____

_____

11. Commit the transaction in **Query1**. What happens in **Query2**?

_____

_____

12. Verify your answer.

■ Part D: Test read uncommitted isolation

1. Execute the following in **Query1**:

```
BEGIN TRAN
UPDATE EmpCount SET COUNT = 8 WHERE Customer = '2198'
```

Because you are updating the **EmpCount** table and the transaction isolation level is set to serializable, an exclusive lock is acquired by the transaction.

2. In **Query2**, execute the following:

```
SELECT * FROM EmpCount
```

3. What happens?

_____

_____

4. Commit the transaction in **Query1**. What happens in **Query2**?

_____

_____

5. In **Query2**, execute the following:

```
SET TRANSACTION ISOLATION LEVEL READ UNCOMMITTED
    RECONFIGURE
```

6. In **Query1**, execute the following:

```
BEGIN TRAN
UPDATE EmpCount SET COUNT = 10 WHERE Customer = '2198'
```

7. In **Query2**, execute the following:

```
SELECT * FROM EmpCount
```

8. What happens? Why?

    _____

    _____

9. What is the **Count** value for **customer 2198**?

    _____

    _____

10. Roll back the transaction in **Query1**. Run a query that returns all rows and columns from **EmpCount** in **Query2**.

11. Has the **Count** value for **customer 2198** changed?

    _____

    _____

12. Explain your result.

    _____

    _____

13. Exit **SQL Server Management Studio**. Do not save changes when prompted.

Project 10.4	Using Transactions
Overview	Transaction processing is the primary activity in many database applications. Transactions are used to ensure that all of the statements complete or that all of the statements are rolled back as if they never ran. It's important that you understand how transactions might interact, what happens when you use different types of transactions, and how some statements can have unexpected consequences.
	The surest way to become familiar with transactions is to use them and observe the results. This includes what you can see while the transaction is still pending and after the transaction is completed, whether committed or rolled back.
Outcomes	After completing this project, you will know how to:
	▲ run transactions and observe the results
	▲ commit and rollback transactions
	▲ use control statements to determine how a transaction is completed
What you'll need	To complete this project, you will need:
	▲ the worksheet below
	▲ a computer running SQL Server 2005 with the sample database Chapter10 attached
Completion time	45 minutes
Precautions	You should be logged in as an administrator at the beginning of the activity steps. Do not make changes to any database other than Chapter10.

■ Part A: Use transactions

1. Launch **SQL Server Management Studio**.
2. Expand **Databases**.
3. Right-click **Chapter10** and select **New Query**. This will be referred to as **Query1** throughout this activity.
4. Right-click **Chapter 10** and select **New Query**. This will be referred to as **Query2** throughout this activity.
5. Right-click **Chapter 10** and select **New Query**. This will be referred to as **Query3** throughout this activity.
6. In **Query1**, execute the following:

```
SET TRANSACTION ISOLATION LEVEL READ UNCOMMITTED
RECONFIGURE
SELECT * FROM OFFICE
```

7. How many rows are returned in the result?

_____

8. In **Query3**, execute the following:

```
BEGIN TRAN
INSERT OFFICE VALUES ('1400', '2332', 100)
INSERT OFFICE VALUES ('1401', '7311', 80)
INSERT OFFICE VALUES ('1402', '7312', 80)
```

9. In **Query1**, execute the following:

```
SELECT * FROM OFFICE
```

10. Explain why the result is different than in step 6.

_____

_____

11. Select **Query3**, open the **File** menu, and select **Close**. A dialog box warns you that there are uncommitted transactions. Click **No** Do not save changes when prompted.

12. In **Query1**, execute the following:

```
SELECT * FROM OFFICE
```

13. Explain why the result is different than in step 9.

_____

_____

14. In **Query2**, execute the following:

```
BEGIN TRAN
INSERT OFFICE VALUES ('1400', '2332', 100)
BEGIN TRAN
INSERT OFFICE VALUES ('1401', '7311', 80)
BEGIN TRAN
INSERT OFFICE VALUES ('1402', '7312', 80)
```

15. Retrieve the value for @@TRANCOUNT. How many open transactions does it show?

    _____

    _____

16. Execute the following:

    ```
    COMMIT TRAN
    ```

17. How many transactions are now open?

    _____

    _____

18. Execute the following:

    ```
    COMMIT TRAN
    ```

19. How many transactions are now open?

    _____

    _____

20. Execute the following:

    ```
    ROLLBACK TRAN
    SELECT * FROM OFFICE
    ```

21. In **Query1**, execute the following:

    ```
    SELECT * FROM OFFICE
    ```

22. Explain the result.

    _____

    _____

23. Execute the following in **Query2**:

```
BEGIN TRAN
SELECT * INTO CUSTOMER_D FROM CUSTOMER
SELECT * INTO CUSTOMER_T FROM CUSTOMER
COMMIT TRAN
```

24. Verify that the tables were created.
25. Execute the following in **Query2**:

```
DELETE CUSTOMER_D
ROLLBACK TRAN
```

26. What happens and why?

_____

_____

27. Execute the following in **Query2**:

```
BEGIN TRAN
DELETE CUSTOMER_T
COMMIT TRAN
ROLLBACK TRAN
```

28. What happens and why?

_____

_____

29. Execute the following in **Query2**:

```
BEGIN TRAN
DROP TABEL CUSTOMER_D
DROP TABEL CUSTOMER_T
```

30. Verify that the transaction is still open.
31. Execute the following in **Query1** (NOT **Query2**):

```
COMMIT TRAN
```

32. What happens and why?

_____

_____

33. Execute the following in **Query2**:

```
BEGIN TRAN
UPDATE CUSTOMER SET CUSTNAME = 'The Home Stores'
WHERE CUSTNUM = '0933'
```

34. Execute the following in **Query1**:

```
BEGIN TRAN
UPDATE CUSTOMER SET CUSTNAME = 'Your Home Stores'
WHERE CUSTNUM = '0933'
COMMIT TRAN
SELECT * FROM CUSTOMER WHERE CUSTNUM = '0933'
```

35. Why won't the command complete?

_____

_____

36. Rollback the transaction in **Query2**. Verify that the commands in **Query1** execute.
37. Exit **SQL Server Management Studio**. Do not save changes when prompted.

Project 10.5	Monitoring Transactions and Clearing Blocked Transactions
Overview	It's important to understand how transaction isolation settings impact concurrent transactions and the use of locks. One way to do this is to observe transactions through available monitoring and management tools. Another is to see how transactions change data and how they can allow or block other transactions' access. Blocking and deadlocks are constant concerns. The more active a database, the more transactions the database engine needs to process, and the more common blocks and deadlocks become. The impact can range from being a slight annoyance to seriously impairing system and application performance. You need to be able to identify blocking transactions and, when necessary, manually clear them. You also need to recognize ways to reduce the possibility of deadlocks.
Outcomes	After completing this project, you will know how to: ▲ monitor transactions ▲ identify blocked transactions ▲ clear blocked transactions
What you'll need	To complete this project, you will need: ▲ a computer with SQL Server 2005 Evaluation Edition installed with the sample Chapter10 database attached ▲ the worksheet below
Completion time	30 minutes
Precautions	You should be logged in as an administrator at the beginning of the project. Do not make changes to any database other than Chapter10.

■ Part A: Manage transactions

1. Launch **SQL Server Management Studio**.
2. Expand **Databases**.
3. Right-click **Chapter10** and select **New Query**. This will be referred to as **Query1** throughout this activity.
4. Right-click **Chapter 10** and select **New Query**. This will be referred to as **Query2** throughout this activity.
5. Execute the following in EACH query window:

```
SET TRANSACTION ISOLATION LEVEL SERIALIZABLE
RECONFIGURE
```

6. In **Object Explorer**, expand **Management**, right-click **Activity Monitor**, and select **View Locks by Object**. The **Activity Monitor** should look similar to Figure 10-1.

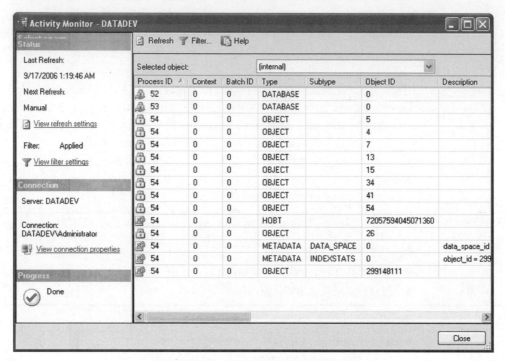

Figure 10-1: Activity Monitor sample

7. Open the **Selected object:** drop-down list. What tables (other than tables in **tempdb**), if any, do you see listed?

_____

_____

8. Execute the following in **Query1**:

```
BEGIN TRAN
UPDATE CUSTOMER SET CUSTNAME = 'Your Home Stores'
WHERE CUSTNUM = '0933'
DELETE OFFICE WHERE OFFNUM >= '2000'
UPDATE SALESPERSON SET SPNAME = 'Dickens'
WHERE SPNUM = '137'
```

9. In **Activity Monitor**, click **Refresh**. In general terms, how does the information displayed change?

_____

_____

10. Open the **Selected object:** drop-down list. You should see the following additional tables listed:

    Chapter10.CUSTOMER
    Chapter10.OFFICE
    Chapter10.SALESPERSON

11. Select **Chapter10.CUSTOMER** from the drop-down list. Scroll until you locate the **Request Mode** column. The value of "**X**" indicates an exclusive lock. What is the process ID associated with this lock?

_____

_____

12. In **Activity Monitor**, under **Select a page**, select **Process Info**. You should see two processes associated with **Chapter10**. What are the process IDs for these processes?

_____

_____

13. Scroll and locate the **Blocked by** and **Blocking** columns. Are any processes identified as blocked? **Tip:** A value of 0 indicates that the process is not blocked or is not blocking any other process.

_____

_____

14. In **Query2**, execute the following:

```
BEGIN TRAN
UPDATE SALESPERSON SET SPNAME = 'Smith'
WHERE SPNUM = '137'
```

15. In **Activity Monitor**, click **Refresh**. What processes are shown as blocked and blocking?

_____

_____

16. Right-click the blocking transaction (with a value of **1** in the Blocking column) and select **Kill process**. Click **Yes** when prompted to verify your action.

17. Has the statement in **Query2** run? Why?

_____

_____

18. Commit the transaction in **Query2**.

19. In **Query1**, execute the following:

```
COMMIT TRAN
```

20. What happens? Why?

_____

_____

21. Exit **SQL Query Manager**. Do not save changes.

11
DATA ACCESS AND SECURITY

PROJECTS

Project 11.1	Understanding Data Access and Security
Overview	Data access and security are broad subjects that are critical to any data environment and database applications. Adding to the potential confusion about security is the fact that different manufacturers have found various ways to address security concerns, with data security evolving as new threats develop.
	A good place to start is ensuring that we're all talking the same language when we discuss security. Commonly accepted definitions of key terms and descriptions of key concepts help move the discussion along. They also help minimize confusion when comparing security designs.
Outcomes	After completing this project, you will know how to: ▲ recognize key access and security terms ▲ describe access and security concepts
What you'll need	To complete this project, you will need: ▲ the worksheet below
Completion time	20 minutes
Precautions	None

The worksheet includes a list of terms on the left and descriptions on the right. Match each term with the description that it most closely matches. You will use all descriptions. Each description can be used only once.

____ Middleware

A. Physical communication line through which data travels

____ Authentication

B. Backup method backing up all changes since the most recent full backup

____ Protocol

C. Security principal used to manage server access and server-level security

____ Connection path

D. Server or database object over which you have control over permission assignments

____ Login

E. Backup method that backs up changes made since the most recent full, differential, or incremental backup

____ User

F. Security system based on Windows authentication and using Windows security principals

____ Incremental

____ Differential

____ Trusted connection

____ Integrated security

____ Failover

____ Disk mirroring

____ Disk striping with parity

____ OLE DB

____ ODBC

____ Securable

G. Database connection based on using the currently logged on Windows user as the basis for authentication

H. Industry-standard data access API

I. Fault-tolerant storage method using two disk drives

J. Process by which a security principal is identified

K. Data access API developed by Microsoft

L. Process of switching control over to a secondary (backup) database server

M. General term referring to software used to tie together components in a multitier application

N. Security principal used to manage database access and database-level security

O. Fault-tolerant storage method requiring three or more disk drives

P. Rules defining data format and transmission, enabling computers to communicate

Project 11.2	Designing for Access and Security
Overview	Some people think of database design as being related to data and nothing else. Although most of the design effort is directly related to data, the data (and the database) would be worthless if no one had access. It can become a liability instead of an asset if you allow unauthorized access because someone can change or steal your data. Access and security design must be considered during the design process. When you deploy your database into a live environment, you need to do so with access and security controls in place.
Outcomes	After completing this project, you will know how to: ▲ include access requirements in a database design ▲ include security requirements in a database design
What you'll need	To complete this project, you will need: ▲ the worksheet below
Completion time	60 minutes
Precautions	None

Below, you are presented with a series of mini case studies. After each case study, answer the design questions.

■ Part A: Case #1

A bookstore wants a database application to support inventory control and point-of-sale invoicing. The same SQL Server 2005 database will be used to support an e-commerce application for sales through a new Web site. The project includes deploying a LAN using Windows Active Directory. The point-of-sale application will run on individual client computers. That is the only access those computers will have to the database server. Inventory control will have clients connecting through graphical query windows and using stored procedures to manage inventory. The Web server will access the database through an application server. The client computers and application server will all be members of the Active Directory domain. Client computers running the point-of-sale application, those doing inventory control, and the application on the application server need to use SQL Server 2005–specific features. You are asked to recommend a programming platform and data access interface for the client and application server applications.

1. How should you configure authentication at the server?

_____

_____

2. How will you meet the interface requirement for clients responsible for inventory control?

_____

_____

3. What should you recommend for accessing the server from the clients running the point-of-sale application?

_____

_____

4. What should you recommend for accessing the server from the application server?

_____

_____

5. In general terms, what must you do to prevent users responsible for inventory control from making changes directly to database tables? Justify your answer.

_____

_____

6. In general terms, what must you do to prevent users responsible for point-of-sale invoicing from making changes directly to database tables?

_____

_____

■ Part B: Case #2

A credit union has nearly 500 employees at two locations in the same city that they identify as their main location and remote location. The two locations share one database hosted on a SQL Server 2005 database server deployed at the main location. The server is configured to support encrypted communication. Computers at the main location are all part of a LAN and members of an Active Directory domain. Computers at the remote location are stand-alone computers with Internet access. Customers can also connect through a secure Web site to manage their own accounts. Security is of special importance for customer connections.

A job task analysis identified, from the context of the database and data application, eight unique task sets and the database access permissions associated with those task sets. An employee might need to perform one or more task sets and will need access to the same task sets unless he or she changes jobs within the credit union.

It is critical that downtime is kept to a minimum. The only protection currently in place is the backup plan. Full backups are run each weekend, and transaction log backups are run twice each day. The company is willing to budget the money necessary to make additional changes.

1. Generally describe the connection path for computers:
   a. At the remote location:

   _____

   b. At the main site:

   _____

   c. For customers:

   _____

2. What would you need to know about the remote connection to make predictions about access performance?

   _____

   _____

3. Describe how you would configure database access security for employee access to database objects to minimize administrative overhead.

   _____

   _____

4. Based on your answer to question 3 in this case study, what would you need to do if an employee changes jobs?

   _____

   _____

5. You want to make sure that the database stays available should a single hard disk fail. What can you do?

   _____

   _____

6. What actions can you take to minimize downtime in case of a serious server hardware failure or loss of multiple hard disks?

   _____

   _____

■ Part C: Case #3

Your company includes data and database administration roles as part of desktop support. You must be able to do database server support tasks from your desk and also test applications as a standard user. Your job requirements sometimes require you to leave your desk for an extended period of time.

Nearly all users, other than support personnel, need the same access permissions to the company database. Support personnel include one individual responsible for ensuring that backups run as scheduled and for changing backup tapes each evening.

You've been tasked with designing a new backup plan. Backups must run fully unattended but must also make it possible to copy the backup taken over the weekend for storage offsite. The new plan should run a full backup each Sunday and an incremental backup each evening, Monday through Saturday. Because of the time required, the full backup can run on Sunday only.

1. How should you configure your access? Include the number and types of security principals involved.

   _____

   _____

2. How should you configure security for the majority of employees? The solution should have minimal administrative overhead involved.

   _____

   _____

3. Based on your answer to question 2 in this case study, what would you need to do if user access requirements change?

   _____

   _____

4. Describe your revised backup plan. Include how it would affect the design if the main server has fault-tolerant disk storage and how you would manage offsite storage.

   _____

   _____

5. How could you change the backup design so it takes less time to restore data after a problem?

   _____

   _____

Project 11.3	Understanding Your Security Environment
Overview	Some aspects of database design are somewhat DBMS neutral. The basic entry/attribute design should be the same for nearly any DBMS. The only differences you're likely to see when you get to tables are due to supported constraints and data types.
	Because they can vary so much, it's important that you know something about how your DBMS implements security features before designing database security. What connectivity options are supported? Does it have a one- or two-tier access hierarchy? Does it support integrated security? Does it have its own authentication system? How are access permissions handled? The list goes on, with each answer directly impacting your security design.
Outcomes	After completing this project, you will know how to:
	▲ explore connectivity options
	▲ explore SQL Server server-level security
	▲ explore SQL Server database-level security
What you'll need	To complete this project, you will need:
	▲ the worksheet below
	▲ a computer running SQL Server 2005 with the Chapter10 sample database attached
	▲ to create a folder named Chap11Data at the root of drive C: and copy the Chapter11.mdf and Chapter11.ldf database files to that folder
Completion time	45 minutes
Precautions	This project is a prerequisite for the remaining projects in this chapter.

■ Part A: Attach a sample database

1. Open the **Start** menu, point to **All Programs**, point to **Microsoft SQL Server 2005**, and then select **SQL Server Management Studio**.
2. If necessary, expand the local server.
3. Right-click **Databases** and select **Attach**.
4. Click **Add**.
5. Locate and select **C:\Chap11Data\Chapter11.mdf**, and then click **OK**.
6. Verify that no errors are reported and click **OK** to attach the database.
7. Expand **Databases**. Verify that **Chapter11** is listed. **NOTE:** Do not exit **SQL Server Management Studio**.

■ **Part B: Explore connectivity settings**

1. Open the **Start** menu, point to **All Programs**, point to **Microsoft SQL Server 2005**, point to **Configuration Tools**, and select **SQL Server Configuration Manager**.
2. Expand **SQL Server 2005 Network Configuration** and select **Protocols for MSSQLSERVER**, which is the database engine service.
3. What protocols are enabled by default? Which protocol would you expect in common with client computers on the same LAN as the database server?

_____

_____

4. Expand **SQL Native Client Configuration** and select **Client Protocols**.
5. Right-click **TCP/IP** and select **Properties**. What is the default port used for **SQL Native Client connections**?

_____

_____

6. Click **Cancel**.
7. Return to the **Configuration Tools** menu and select **SQL Server Surface Area Configuration.**
8. Click **Surface Area Configuration for Services and Connections**.
9. If necessary, expand **MSSQLSERVER** and expand **Database Engine**. Select **Remote Connections**, as shown in Figure 11-1.

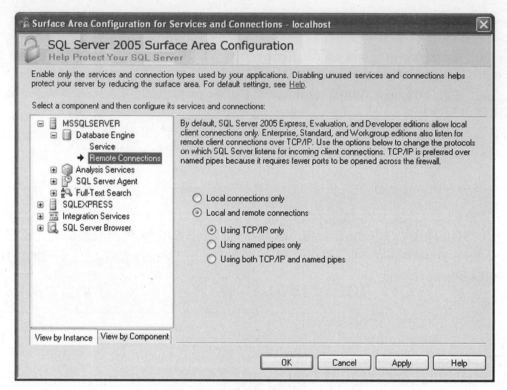

Figure 11-1: Remote Connections settings

10. Figure 11-1 shows the default configuration setting. How would you disable remote connections?

_____

_____

11. Click **Cancel**. Exit **Surface Area Configuration**.

■ Part C: Explore server security by reviewing SQL Server Management Studio server properties

1. In **Object Explorer**, right-click your local server and select **Properties**.
2. Select **Connections**, as shown in Figure 11-2.

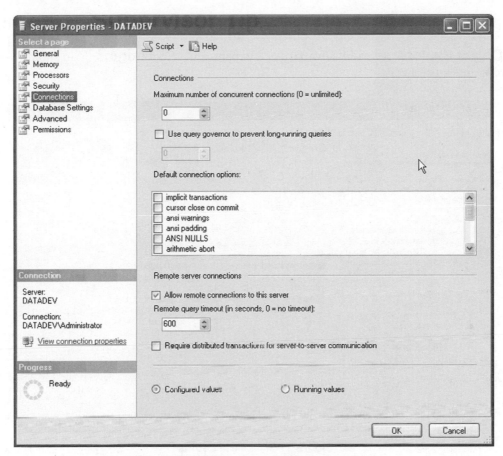

Figure 11-2: Server Connections properties

3. How many concurrent connections are currently allowed?

   _____

   _____

4. What is the potential drawback of limiting concurrent connections?

   _____

   _____

5. Select **Security**. What auditing parameters are available?

   _____

   _____

6. Click **Cancel**. Do not exit **SQL Server Management Studio**.

■ Part D: Explore server security by reviewing the current server logins

1. In **Object Explorer**, expand **Security** and expand and select **Logins**. You should see a list similar to Figure 11-3.

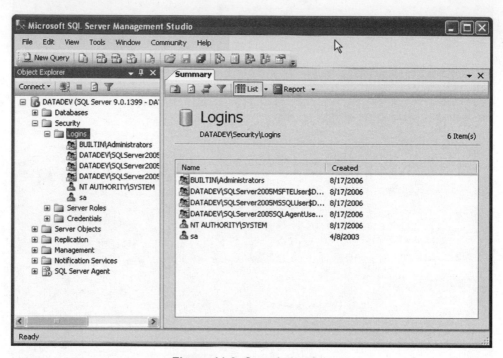

Figure 11-3: Sample Logins

2. Right-click **BUILTIN/Administrators**, which was added during SQL Server installation, and select **Properties**. What is the default database for this login?

_____

3. Select **Server Roles**. With which server roles, if any, does this login belong?

_____

_____

4. Click **Cancel** to close the login properties.
5. Expand **Server Roles**. These are the default server roles for managing server-level security. You cannot create additional server roles.
6. To view a role's members, right-click the role, select **Properties**, and then click **Cancel** to close the properties without making any changes. Review the members of all of the server roles.

■ Part E: Explore database security by reviewing current database users

1. If not already expanded, expand **Databases**, expand **Chapter11**, and then expand **Security**.

2. Expand and select **Users**, as shown in Figure 11-4.

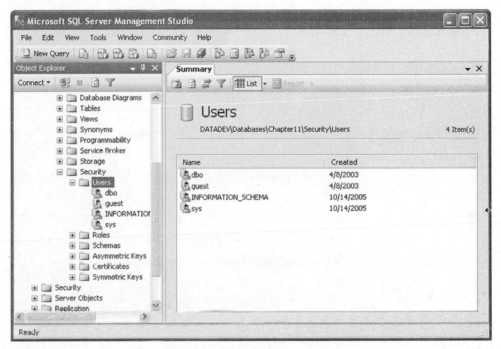

Figure 11-4: Database Users

3. Right-click **dbo** and select **Properties**.

4. Scroll through the roles list. To what roles does the user belong? Why isn't it necessary to include the public role in this list?

_____

_____

5. Click **Cancel**.

6. Display the properties for **guest**. What, if any, is the associated login? What role membership is shown?

_____

_____

7. Click **Cancel**.

■ Part F: Review database roles

1. Expand and select **Roles**.
2. Expand **Database Roles**.
3. Right-click **public** and select **Properties**. Why do you think there are no members listed?

   _____

   _____

4. Click **Securables**. What securables and permissions are listed?

   _____

   _____

5. Click **Cancel**.
6. Right-click **db_owner** and select **Properties**. Which users, if any, are listed as members?

   _____

   _____

7. Why doesn't the role include a **Securables** page?

   _____

   _____

8. Click **Cancel**.
9. Review the properties for all database roles. Which roles let you change the default permissions?

   _____

   _____

10. Exit **SQL Server Management Studio**.

Project 11.4	Managing Security Principals
Overview	The security principals can vary by DBMS. In a two-tier security system, like that used by SQL Server 2005, one set of security principals controls server security and the other set controls database security. Security is managed separately for each database.
	In a single-tier system, server and database security are managed using the same security principals. A security system of this type is often less flexible than a two-tier system.
	Another concern is how authentication is managed. Most modern DBMSs support integrated security, basing database server security on Windows security, as well as a database server-based authentication method.
	How secure your databases are depends on how well you design and implement security. The security principals are the foundation of your security.
Outcomes	After completing this project, you will know how to:
	▲ set authentication options
	▲ create and manage logins
	▲ create and manage database users
What you'll need	To complete this project, you will need:
	▲ a computer running SQL Server 2005 with the sample database Chapter11 attached
Completion time	45 minutes
Precautions	Limit your modifications to those explicitly called for in this project. If your database server is part of a network, do not make any changes to Windows users without first checking with your database administrator.
	A portion of this exercise cannot be completed if the database server is also configured as an Active Directory domain server. These steps are clearly identified and will not prevent you from completing the rest of the project.
	This project is required for Project 11.5.

■ **Part A: Manage authentication**

1. Launch **SQL Server Management Studio**.
2. Right-click your server instance and select **Properties**.
3. Select **Security**.
4. Under **Server authentication**, select **SQL Server and Windows Authentication mode**.

5. Under **Login auditing**, select **Both failed and successful logins**. What is the potential downside of this configuration for an active server with a large number of logins?

_____

_____

6. Verify that your settings look like those in Figure 11-5.

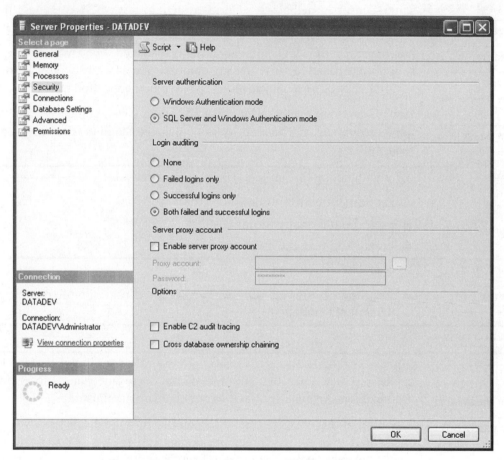

Figure 11-5: Authentication and login settings

7. Click **OK** to save your settings.
8. You need to stop and restart the server to apply the changes. Right-click your server instance and select **Stop**. Click **Yes** both times when prompted to verify your action.
9. Right-click the server instances and select **Start**. Click **Yes** when prompted to verify your action.
10. It may be necessary to restart **SQL Server Agent**. Right-click **SQL Server Agent** and, if the command is available, select **Start**. Click **Yes** when prompted to verify your action.

■ Part B: Manage logins

1. Expand **Security**. Expand and select **Logins**.
2. Right-click **Logins** and select **New Login**. Configure the login properties as given in Table 11-1. Leave settings not specified at their default values.

Table 11-1: New login

Parameter	Setting
Login name	Good
Login type	SQL Server authentication
Password	P*55word
Confirm password	P*55word
Enforce password expiration	*Clear check*

3. Click **OK** to create the login.
4. Create a login with the settings set forth in Table 11-2.

Table 11-2: New login

Parameter	Setting
Login name	Bad
Login type	SQL Server authentication
Password	P*55word
Confirm password	P*55word
Enforce password expiration	*Clear check*

5. Create a login with the settings set forth in Table 11-3.

Table 11-3: New login

Parameter	Setting
Login name	Defaulter
Login type	SQL Server authentication
Password	P*55word
Confirm password	P*55word
Enforce password expiration	*Clear check*
Default database	Chapter11

NOTE: Parts C and D cannot be completed if your database server is also configured as a domain controller.

■ Part C: Create a Windows local user account

1. Open the **Control Panel** and launch **Administrative Tools**. **NOTE:** If **Control Panel** is in **Category** view, switch to **Classic** view.
2. From the **Administrative Tools** window, launch **Computer Management**.
3. Expand **Local Users and Groups** and select **Users**.
4. Right-click **Users** and select **New User**.
5. Complete the user parameters as listed in Table 11-4. Leave the remaining fields at their default values.

Table 11-4: New Windows user

Parameter	Setting
User name	SQLUser
Full name	Generic User
Password	P*55word
Confirm password	P*55word
User must change password at next logon	*Clear check*

6. Click **Create**, and then click **Close** to exit the **New User** dialog box.
7. Exit **Computer Management** and close the **Administrative Tools** window.

■ Part D: Create a Windows authentication login account

1. In **Management Studio Object Explorer**, right-click **Logins** and select **New Login**.
2. **Windows authentication** is selected by default. In the **Login-New** dialog box, click **Search**.
3. In the **Select User or Group** dialog box, click **Advanced**.
4. Click **Find Now**.
5. Locate and select **SQLUser**, and then click **OK**.
6. In the **Select User or Group** dialog box, click **OK**.
7. Select **Chapter11** as the default database, then click **OK** to create the login.

■ **Part E: View the CREATE command used to create a login**

1. Right-click **Good** and select **Script Login as**, then **CREATE To**, and then **New Query Editor Window**.

2. Review the **CREATE** statement in the query window, as shown in Figure 11-6.

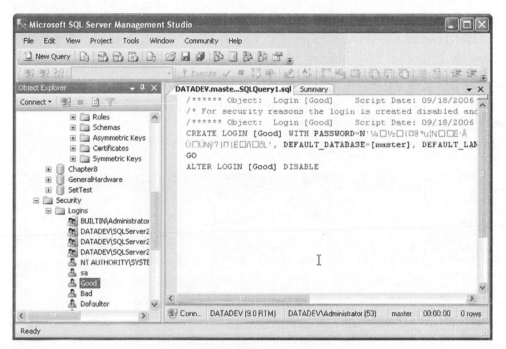

Figure 11-6: CREATE LOGIN statement

3. What prevents someone from using this to retrieve the login's password?

    _____

    _____

4. Close the query window. Do not save changes when prompted.

■ **Part F: Manage database users**

1. Expand **Databases**, expand **Chapter11**, expand **Security**, and select and expand **Users**.
2. Right-click **Users** and select **New User**.
3. Type **GoodUser** as the user name.
4. Click the browse button (**...**) to the right of the login name field.
5. Click **Browse**.
6. Check **Good**, and then click **OK**.
7. Click **OK**.

8. Type **dbo** as the **Default schema**.

9. Click **OK**. To what roles, if any, should the user currently belong?

    _____

    _____

10. Right-click **Users** and select **New User**.

11. Type **BadUser** as the user name.

12. Type **Bad** as the login name and **dbo** as the default schema.

13. Click **OK** to create the user.

14. Right-click **GoodUser** and select **Script User as**, then **CREATE To**, and then **New Query Editor Window**.

15. You should see a **CREATE** statement similar to the one shown in Figure 11-7.

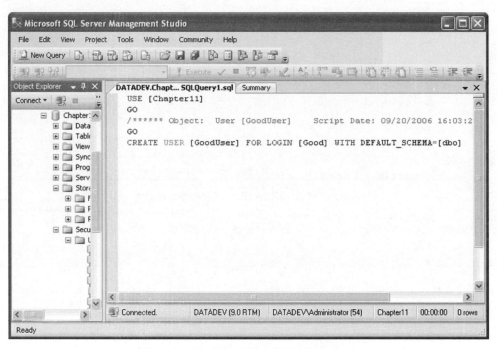

Figure 11-7: CREATE USER statement

16. Close the query window. Do not save changes when prompted.

■ **Part G: Create a user from the command line**

1. Right-click **Chapter11** and select **New Query**.

2. Execute the following

```
CREATE USER DefaultType FOR LOGIN Defaulter
WITH DEFAULT_SCHEMA=dbo
```

3. Right-click **Users** and select **Refresh**. Verify that **DefaultType** is listed as a database user.
4. Exit **SQL Server Management Studio**. Do not save any open query windows when prompted.

Project 11.5	Managing Permissions
Overview	Configuring authentication and server connectivity is only part of the overall security plan. You must also determine what access is required to the data and how you can manage that access.
	As a general rule of thumb, you can reduce the administrative overhead if you can manage access to the general and make allowance for the specific. Whenever possible, base access security on groups of users rather than on individual users. Following the same idea, base security on groups or types (or categories) of objects rather than individual database objects. The level of granularity within database object permissions, as well as whether (and how) you can identify groups of users or objects, varies somewhat by DBMS. However, at least some of what you learn working with one DBMS can usually be applied to other DBMSs.
Outcomes	After completing this project, you will know how to:
	▲ manage server role membership
	▲ create and manage database roles and role membership
	▲ set object-level permissions
What you'll need	To complete this project, you will need:
	▲ a computer with SQL Server 2005 Evaluation Edition installed with the sample Chapter11 database attached
	▲ to have completed Project 11.4 (except those steps that cannot be completed on a domain controller) before starting this project
Completion time	90 minutes
Precautions	Do not make database or database object permission changes to any database other than Chapter11.

■ Part A: Manage server permissions

1. Launch **SQL Server Management Studio**.

2. If necessary, expand your server, expand **Security**, and expand **Server Roles**.

3. Expand **roles**, right-click **sysadmin** (membership to which makes a login a server administrator), and select **Properties**.

4. Click **Add**.

5. Click **Browse** in the **Select Logins** dialog box.

6. Check **Good**, and then click **OK**.

7. Click **OK**. Verify that **Good** is listed as a role member.

8. Using the steps already described, add the login **Defaulter** as a member of the **dbcreator** role.

9. Open the properties for the login **Bad**, change the default database to **Chapter11**, and then save the change.

■ Part B: Test server permissions

1. Open the **File** menu and select **Disconnect Object Explorer**.

2. Open the **File** menu and select **Connect Object Explorer**.

3. Select **SQL Server Authentication**.

4. Type **Good** as the login, enter the password, and then click **Connect**.

5. What is the potential risk in checking **Remember password**?

   _____

   _____

6. Expand **Security** and select **Logins**. You should see all of the logins listed.

7. Right-click **Defaulter** and select **Properties**. Change the password to something you can easily remember and save the change. Can you modify the login properties?

   _____

   _____

8. Why do you have rights to modify logins?

   _____

   _____

■ **Part C: Disconnect and reconnect as a different login**

1. Disconnect the current **Object Explorer**.
2. Connect using the SQL Server login **Bad**.

■ **Part D: Test server permissions again**

1. Expand **Security** and **Logins**. What users do you see listed?

   _____

   _____

2. Why aren't you able to see other logins?

   _____

   _____

3. Right-click **Logins** and select **New Login**. Create a new login named **Extra** with a password of **P*55word** and click **OK**. What happens?

   _____

   _____

4. Close any open warning or dialog boxes. Right-click **Databases** and select **New Database**.
5. Create a database named **Bad_Test**. Can you create a database when connected as this login?

   _____

   _____

■ **Part E: Test permissions for login Defaulter**

1. Disconnect and reconnect as **Defaulter**. Remember to use the new password.
2. Attempt to create a new login named **NewTest**. Can you create a login? Explain your answer.

   _____

   _____

3. Attempt to create a new database named **Defaulter_DB**. Why can you create a database? Explain your answer.

_____

_____

4. Delete the database. What happens?

_____

_____

5. Disconnect and reconnect using Windows authentication.

■ Part F: Test current permissions

1. Right-click **Chapter11** and select **New Query**. Verify that **Chapter11** is selected at the current database.
2. Execute the following:

```
SELECT * FROM CUSTOMER
```

3. What happens?

_____

_____

4. Execute the following:

```
DELETE EmpCount WHERE Customer = '2198'
```

5. What happens?

_____

_____

6. Execute the following:

```
SELECT USER
```

7. What database user are you connected as?

    _____

    _____

8. Open the **Query** menu and select **Connection**, and then **Change Connection**.
9. Choose **SQL Server Authentication** and connect as **Good**.
10. What is the default database and why?

    _____

    _____

11. Change the current database to **Chapter11**.
12. Execute the following:

    ```
    SELECT USER
    ```

    You connect as the same user because this user is configured as a database owner and because the login did not default to this database.
13. Execute the following and verify that both commands run without error:

    ```
    SELECT * FROM CUSTOMER
    DELETE EmpCount WHERE Customer = '1525'
    ```

14. Change the query connection and connect as **Bad**.
15. What is the current user name?

    _____

    _____

16. What is the current database? Why?

    _____

    _____

17. Change the current database to **Chapter11**.
18. Execute the following:

    ```
    SELECT * FROM CUSTOMER
    ```

19. What happens?

_____

_____

20. Change the query connection and connect as **Bad**.
21. What is the current user name?

_____

_____

22. What is the current database? Why?

_____

_____

23. Change the current database to **Chapter11**.
24. Execute the following:

```
SELECT * FROM CUSTOMER
```

25. What happens?

_____

_____

26. Close any open query windows. Do not save changes when prompted.

■ Part G: Manage database permissions by defining public role permissions

1. Expand **Databases**, **Chapter11**, and **Security**.
2. Expand **Roles** and select **Database Roles**.
3. Right-click **Public** and select **Properties**.
4. Select **Securables**.
5. Under **Securables**, click **Add**.
6. In the **Add Objects** dialog box, select **All objects of the types** and click **OK**.
7. In the **Select Object Types** dialog box, check **Tables** and click **OK**.
8. For each table, select the table under **Securables**, and under the explicit permissions list, check **Insert**, **Select**, and **Update**.
9. Click **OK** to save changes to **Securables** and close the role properties.

■ Part H: Create a custom role

1. Right-click **Database Roles** and select **New Database Role**.
2. Name the role **Extra Permissions**.
3. Select **Securables**.
4. Under **Securables**, click **Add**.
5. Leave **Specific objects** selected and click **OK**.
6. Click **Object Types,** check **Tables**, and click **OK**.
7. Click **Browse,** check the **CUSTOMER**, **EmpCount**, and **PRODUCT** tables, and then click **OK**. The **Select Objects** dialog box should look like the example in Figure 11-8.

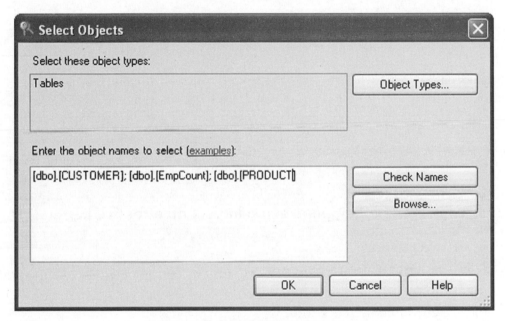

Figure 11-8: Select Objects dialog box

8. Click **OK**.
9. For each table, select the table, and check **Grant** for **Alter** and **Delete**.
10. Click **OK** to save the changes.

■ Part I: Test database permissions granted through roles

1. Right-click **Chapter11** and select **New Query**. Change the connection to **Defaulter**. Retrieve the current user to verify the change.
2. Execute both statements below.

```
SELECT * FROM CUSTOMER
DELETE EmpCount WHERE Customer = '0933'
```

3. Which statements, if any, run without error? Why?

_____

_____

4. Right-click **Extra Permissions** and select **Properties**.
5. Under **Role members**, click **Add**.
6. Type **DefaultType** as thc object name, click **Check Names**, and then click **OK**. Verify that the user is listed.
7. Click **OK** to save the property changes.
8. In the query window, execute the following:

```
DELETE EmpCount WHERE Customer = '0933'
```

9. What happens? Explain why.

_____

_____

■ Part J: Test user explicit permission impact on effective permissions

1. Expand and select **Users**.
2. Right-click **BadUser** and select **Properties**.
3. Click **Securables**.
4. Under the **Securables** list, click **Add**.
5. Leave **Specific objects** selected and click **OK**.
6. Select **Table** as the object type and the **EmpCount** table, and then click **OK** to save the selection.
7. Check **Deny** for the **Delete** permission for **EmpCount** and click **OK**.
8. Add **BadUser** as a member to the **Extra Permissions** role.
9. Change connection in the query window to **Bad**. Retrieve the current user to verify the change.
10. Execute the following:

```
DELETE EmpCount WHERE Customer = '0121'
```

11. The user was granted the **Delete** permission through membership in the **Extra Permissions** role. Why did the command fail?

_____

_____

12. Exit **SQL Server Management Studio**. Do not save changes when prompted.

Project 11.6	Managing Backups
Overview	Backups are a critical part of any database design and security plan. In most situations, you will want to configure periodic backups to run on regular schedules with little or no operator interaction required. A usual exception to this is that special or additional backups are sometimes needed to support off-site storage requirements (if not part of the periodic backup plan), bulk import, or maintenance requirements. The backup types and backup options supported by SQL Server 2005 are typical of many PC-based DBMSs. It's important to be familiar with the specific backup procedures supported by your selected DBMS.
Outcomes	After completing this project, you will know how to: ▲ back up database data ▲ restore database data
What you'll need	To complete this project, you will need: ▲ a computer with SQL Server 2005 Evaluation Edition installed with the sample Chapter11 database attached
Completion time	30 minutes
Precautions	None

■ Part A: Back up a database

1. Create a folder named **Backup Test** at the root of drive **C:**.
2. Launch **SQL Server Management Studio**. Connect using **Windows authentication**.
3. Expand **Databases**.
4. Right-click **Chapter11** and select **Tasks** and then **Back up**.
5. Under **Destination**, click **Remove** to remove the default destination.
6. Click **Add**. Type the following as the destination: **C:\Backup Test\Backup.bak**.
7. Click **OK** twice.
8. Click **Options**.

9. Under **Overwrite media**, select **Overwrite all existing backup sets**.

10. Click **OK**.

11. Click **OK** when the backup is reported as complete.

12. Launch **My Computer**, navigate to **C:\Backup Test**, and verify that the backup file was created.

■ Part B: Test restore and recovery

1. In **SQL Server Management Studio**, right-click **Chapter11** and open a new query window.

2. Drop the **EmpCount table**, then close the query window. Do not save changes when prompted.

3. Expand **Tables** and verify that the table is not listed.

4. Right-click **Chapter11** and select **Tasks**, then **Restore**, and then **Database**.

5. Verify that the backup you just ran is selected, as shown in Figure 11-9.

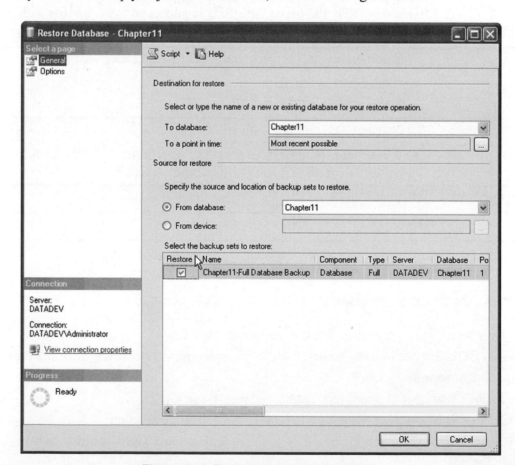

Figure 11-9: Restore Database dialog box

6. Select **Options**.

7. Check **Overwrite the existing database**. Leave the remaining settings at default.

8. Click **OK**.

9. When a dialog box reports that the restore is complete, click **OK**.

10. Expand tables and verify that **EmpCount** is listed. This shows you that the restore was successful.

11. Exit **SQL Server Management Studio**.

12

SUPPORTING DATABASE APPLICATIONS

PROJECTS

Project 12.1	Understanding Data Configurations
Overview	It's important to understand terms related to data configurations, which include distributed operations, data filtering, and data replication requirements. You also need to recognize terms related to application components used in the different data environments.
Outcomes	After completing this project, you will know how to: ▲ identify terms related to data configurations ▲ identify terms related to distributed operations ▲ identify terms related to data replication
What you'll need	To complete this project, you will need: ▲ the worksheet below
Completion time	30 minutes
Precautions	None

The worksheet below includes a list of terms on the left and descriptions on the right. Match each term with the description that it most closely matches. You will use all descriptions. Each description can be used only once.

___	Horizontal partitioning	A. Filtering a data table by column
___	Vertical partitioning	B. Elapsed time required for a Web server's response to display in the client's browser
___	Database persistence	C. Data query that retrieves data from multiple databases
___	Proxy server	D. Replication configuration that copies an entire table to the destination server
___	Query cache	E. Data configuration with data located on a database server, on the local client computer, and on a mainframe computer
___	Distributed query	F. Filtering a data table by row
___	MS DTC	G. Transaction processing method used with distributed transactions
___	Snapshot replication	H. Act of caching queries at the Web server or a proxy server in an Internet-based application

_____ Change replication

_____ Transactional replication

_____ Two-phase commit

_____ Response time

_____ Latency

_____ Two-tier environment

_____ Three-tier environment

I. Time between when data changes and when the change is replicated to the destination server

J. Replication configuration where changed rows in a source table are written to the destination

K. Data configuration with data located on a database server and on the local client computer

L. Area of dedicated memory associated with the Web server that is used to temporarily hold query results

M. Replication configuration where completed transactions are copied to the destination database's transaction log

N. Microsoft software component that manages distributed transactions

O. Support server that, among other functions, can cache copies of recently retrieved Web pages

Project 12.2	Designing Data Environments
Overview	The data environment is a key part of application design and implementation. Data access design is directly impacted by data location. Centralized data configurations are the easiest to manage. Distributed data configurations, those with multiple databases, are more difficult to manage but also more flexible. Distributed data configurations bring with them the need to support distributed queries and transactions. Many distributed data configurations also include replication requirements, with replication used to keep remote copies consistent and up to date. Designing the data environment is an important part of overall data and database design. Design decisions will depend on factors such as the physical locations of data consumers, the communication infrastructure available, security concerns, and performance targets.
Outcomes	After completing this project, you will know how to: ▲ recognize centralized data requirements ▲ recognize distributed data requirements
What you'll need	To complete this project, you will need: ▲ the worksheet below
Completion time	60 minutes
Precautions	None

Below, you are presented with a series of mini case studies. Answer the questions following each case study.

■ Part A: Case #1

A custom bakery has four shops in St. Louis. They take walk-in and phone orders. Phone orders are taken at the downtown location and passed on to the location nearest the customer. Most custom orders are for delivery rather than pick-up. They want to be able to take orders over the Internet within 6 months.

Each shop is configured with its own LAN. The shops are connected through the Internet with a secure, full-time, high-bandwidth connection. Each location connects to the Internet through a firewall. The network administrator, who also handles user support for the bakery, works out of the downtown shop. Because the downtown shop is the main location, it tends to have the most computer problems. They have college students working as part-time technicians at the other shops to assist with fixing minor problems, but they have limited experience or expertise.

The bakery wants to start using a database to track store records. The first phase will be putting customer, inventory, accounting, and other store records in the database. Data is currently stored in Microsoft Access databases and Excel spreadsheets. During the second phase, they plan to post pictures of custom projects for advertising purposes and as suggestions for customers. Queries retrieving these pictures need to be optimized.

The database design calls for queries of outstanding customer orders made to the remote shops to return orders assigned to that shop only. The same applies to queries of supplies and equipment. You should be able to run queries from the downtown location to return information related either to just that location or to the business as a whole.

Database management will be handled in-house. All of the application programming is being contracted out. Someone will be hired to manage the Web site before it goes live. You want to keep expenses related to the project to a minimum. Hardware resource requirements should be minimized on any computers purchased to support the solution. You also want to minimize the management overhead required by the solution.

1. Describe the type of data environment you would use and why.

_____

_____

_____

_____

_____

2. What, if any, replication requirements are needed to support the design? Explain your answer.

_____

_____

_____

_____

_____

3. Describe two table design options for meeting the query requirements described. Include any additional database objects required by the solution. Explain how to keep access simple for the queries.

_____

_____

_____

_____

_____

_____

4   The Web server should not connect directly to the database server. What components will be
     required to deploy the Web site and to protect the database server from unauthorized access
     from the Internet?

_____

_____

_____

_____

_____

_____

■ Part B: Case #2

Several smaller farm cooperatives are joining together to form a United States–wide agricultural
    coop. Each state capital will have a management office and a database for tracking product
    inventories and futures records for that state. Purchase and sales records will be maintained at
    a central database in the main office in Washington, DC. In addition to purchases and sales,
    the Washington office will track all coop member and customer records, and will be
    responsible for accounting, payroll, and coop payments to individual farms. Data maintained
    on each database are unique to that database.

Most of the direct contact with farms and customers will be through field representatives. Any
    field representative can post purchase and sales records, including transactions that include
    farms and products in multiple states. Each field representative is assigned to a specific state
    office and connects to that office through the Internet. Most field representatives do not have
    a personal office, instead working primarily out of their homes and vehicles. Some have been
    loaned space for use as an office on local farms.

Farmers can also interact with the coop through a public Web site. They can browse the public
    information or, if a member, log in for access to a members-only area. You must log in to
    view current and futures price information or to make purchases from a members-only e-
    commerce site. Each state hosts its own home page and local informational pages, and all
    state sites have links to the national site maintained out of the Washington office.

1.   Describe the type of data environment that should be used any why.

_____
_____
_____
_____
_____
_____

2   Describe replication needs (if any). Justify your answer.

_____
_____
_____
_____
_____
_____

3. Describe distributed transaction needs (if any). Justify your answer.

_____
_____
_____
_____
_____
_____

4. In terms of resource requirements and use at each location, what are the advantages of the data model described here?

_____
_____
_____
_____

5. In general terms, describe the communication paths used to support this configuration.

_____

_____

_____

_____

_____

_____

6. Field representatives complain that some, even within the same state, get better performance when accessing data than others. Discuss the most likely cause.

_____

_____

_____

_____

_____

_____

■ Part C: Case #3

The company you work for makes its money from vacation and leisure. It owns and operates cruise ships and vacation resorts. Vacationers can book a cruise, resort stay, or complete vacation package, including travel, car rental, stays at other hotels, and additional items as necessary. Your company acts as the point of contact for resolving any problems a customer might have.

Customer records, vacation itineraries, and similar information are maintained at the main office in Las Vegas. Each resort and ship is managed as a separate financial entity and has a database for that purpose. That includes all financial and operational information, such as employees, resources, and inventories. Each also has reservation information for customers staying there. They must call Las Vegas for itinerary changes for travel or changes affecting other locations. Updates between Las Vegas and other locations are made nightly through an EDI application. The only information sent to Las Vegas is local reservation changes and periodic financial summaries.

You've been brought in to restructure the system. Each location will still be managed as a separate financial entity, but it must be possible to view and modify itinerary information from any location. The accounting department must be able to retrieve financial summary information on an as-needed basis. Telephone sales and customer support operations will be maintained in Las Vegas. Customers must also be able to call up their own itinerary and request changes online. Data connections to cruise ships and to some resort locations are unreliable, so there may be a delay in updates made in one location being incorporated into the consolidated customer records in Las Vegas. It's important that updates be made at all locations, but these are not considered to be especially time sensitive.

Most database problems and all periodic maintenance will be handled locally. When the new system is in place, it is important that there be centralized oversight of the system as a whole. The database administration staff in Las Vegas will periodically review data, database, and server management and configuration settings.

1. Describe the projected data environment after the restructuring is complete. Include what data is stored where and instances of duplicate data, if any, in the system.

2. Describe, in general terms, how the system is designed to handle changes to customer itineraries.

3. In general, what are the requirements, if any, for distributed transactions and distributed queries?

_____

_____

_____

_____

_____

4. What are the requirements, if any, for replication?

_____

_____

_____

_____

_____

5. What are the potential data concerns related to replication?

_____

_____

_____

_____

_____

6. How does the communication infrastructure affect latency?

_____

_____

_____

_____

_____

7. Describe how database administration will be managed.

_____

_____

_____

_____

_____

_____

8. What potential administration problems are posed by the data communication infrastructure?

_____

_____

_____

_____

_____

_____

9. In general terms, explain how data requirements for Internet access by customers should be met.

_____

_____

_____

_____

_____

_____

Project 12.3	Working in a Distributed Environment
Overview	Most of the activities and operations needed to support a distributed environment are effectively the same as for a centralized environment. The difference is that multiple servers are involved. This means that some operations must be run as distributed operations. Data communication becomes a significant issue that can affect access and performance. Security can also be an issue because of servers located on different networks and possibly configured for different types of authentication. You can even have to deal with completely different DBMSs. You can have a physically local environment that must be managed as a distributed environment. This happens when you have multiple servers deployed on the same LAN. This could be due to security requirements such as the need to configure security differently on some servers to provide a more secure environment. It could also be due to having to support a heterogeneous data environment, such as you might have while transitioning to a different primary DBMS.
Outcomes	After completing this project, you will know how to: ▲ create a distributed data environment ▲ manage database servers in a distributed environment
What you'll need	To complete this project, you will need: ▲ a computer running SQL Server 2005 ▲ the installation software for SQL Server 2005 Evaluation Edition ▲ to create two folders named Chap12Local and Chap12Remote at the root of drive C:. Copy Local12.mdf and Local12.ldf from the student CD to C:\Chap12Local, and Remote12.mdf and Remote12.ldf to C:\Chap12Remote
Completion time	90 minutes
Precautions	Be sure to follow the installation instructions closely to ensure that your data environment is configured correctly. You must be logged on as an administrator to complete this project.

■ Part A: Create a distributed environment by installing SQL Server 2005 Evaluation Edition

1. Insert the evaluation edition CD and let it autorun to start the installation.
2. Click **Server components**, **tools**, **Books Online**, and **samples**.
3. Check **I accept the licensing terms and conditions** and click **Next**. There will be a short delay while the installation prerequisite setup support files install.
4. Click **Next**.

5. When the **Installation Wizard** launches, click **Next**.

6. Review the system configuration check and click **Next**.

7. Leave the registration information at default and click **Next**.

8. Check **SQL Server Database Services** and click **Next**. Why don't you need to install workstation components or **Book Online** on this computer to have them available?

_____

_____

9. Click **Advanced**.

10. Click **Browse**. Set the installation path to **C:\Program Files\ Remote SQL Server** and click **OK**.

11. Click **Next**.

12. Select **Named instance** and name the server instance **Remote**. Click **Next**.

13. Select to use the **Local system** account as the **Service Account** and to start **SQL Server Agent** automatically, as shown in Figure 12-1, then click **Next**.

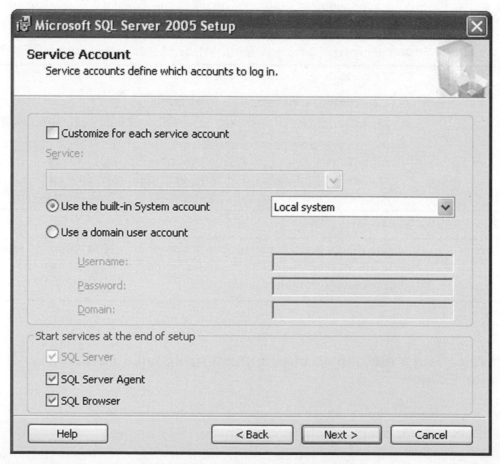

Figure 12-1: Service Account settings

14. Select **Mixed Mode** authentication, enter the password as **P*55word**, and click **Next.**

15. Leave the collation settings at default and click **Next**.

16. Leave error and usage report settings at default (not checked) and click **Next**.

17. Review your installation choices and click **Install**. There will be a delay while the installation runs.

18. When setup is complete, click **Next**, and then **Finish**.

19. Shut down and restart your computer.

■ Part B: Configure a distributed environment by configuring SQL Server Management Studio to register a "remote" server for management

1. Open **SQL Server Management Studio**.

2. Select **View** and then **Registered Servers**.

3. Expand **Database Engine** to view current registered servers.

4. Right-click **Database Engine** and select **New** and then **Server Registration**.

5. Open the **Server name** drop-down list and choose **<Browse for more>**.

6. Under **Local Servers,** expand **Database Engine** and choose *servername*\REMOTE to choose the simulated remote server and click **OK**. The **New Server Registration** dialog box should look similar to Figure 12-2.

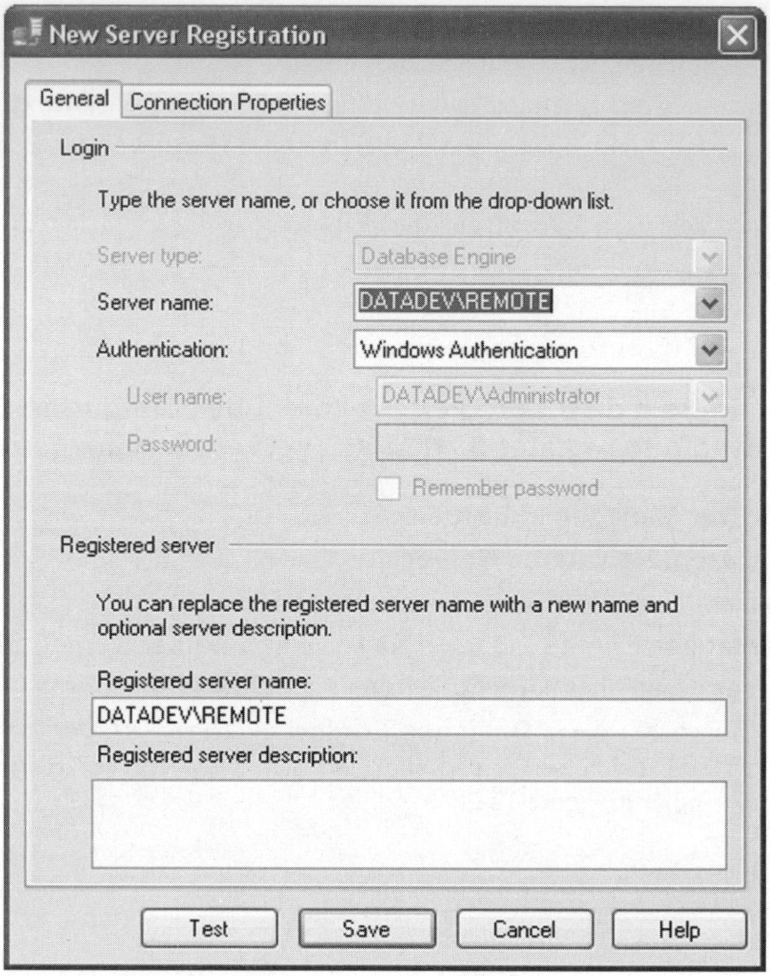

Figure 12-2: New Server Registration dialog box

7. When would you use the **Network Servers** tab in **Microsoft SQL Server Management Studio** to locate the server?

    _____

    _____

8. Click **Test** to test the connection. Click **OK** to close the dialog box reporting a successful connection.

9. Click **Save**.

10. Verify that the server is listed in the **Registered Servers** window, as shown in Figure 12-3.

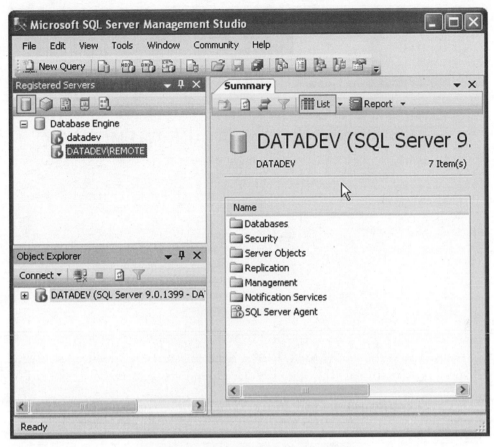

Figure 12-3: Registered Servers window

11.   Close the **Registered Servers** window.

■ Part C: Connect to the registered "remote" server

1.   Select **File** and then **Connect Object Explorer**.

2.   Select the **REMOTE** instance from the **Server Name** drop-down. **Tip:** You may need to select **<Browse for more>** and select the server from the **Database Engine** list.

3.   Click **Connect**. The server instance should be listed in **Object Explorer**, as shown in Figure 12-4.

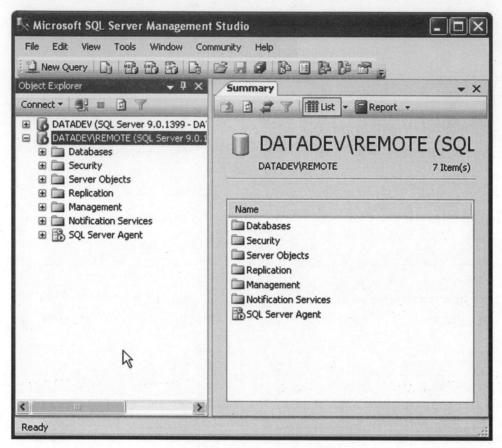

Figure 12-4: Connected server

■ Part D: Attach the sample database for the default instance

1. Expand your default instance.
2. Right-click **Databases** and select **Attach**.
3. Click **Add**. Locate and select **C:\Chap12Local\Local12.mdf**, and then click **OK**.
4. Click **OK** to attach the database.
5. Expand **Databases** and verify that **Local12** is listed.
6. Repeat the procedure in steps 1–5 to attach **C:\Chap12Remote\Remote12.mdf** to the **REMOTE** instance. Verify that **Remote12** is listed under **Databases** when finished.

NOTE: Throughout the rest of this exercise, the default SQL Server instance will be referred to as your local server and the named instance REMOTE as your remote server, to simulate working in a distributed environment.

■ **Part E: Practice centralized management by comparing server security configurations**

1. Under your local server, expand **Security**, and then expand and select **Logins**. Review the list of logins.

2. Under your remote server, expand **Security**, and then expand and select **Logins**. In general, how does this list compare to the list on the local server?

    _____

    _____

3. What does this tell you about security management for different servers managed in the same instance of **SQL Server Management Studio**?

    _____

    _____

4. Expand **Databases** for each of the instances. In general, how do the user database lists compare?

    _____

    _____

■ **Part F: Configure both servers to require distributed transactions**

1. Right-click your local server and select **Properties**.
2. Select **Connections**.
3. Check **Require distributed transactions for server-to-server communication**.
4. Click **OK** to save the property changes.
5. Repeat steps 1–4 for your remote server.

■ **Part G: Stop and start database servers**

Complete the following steps for both servers:

1. Right-click the server and select **Stop**. When each dialog box prompts you to verify your action, click **Yes**.
2. Right-click the server and select **Start**. Click **Yes** to verify your action when prompted.
3. Right-click **SQL Server Agent** and select **Start**. Click **Yes** to verify your action when prompted.
4. Exit **SQL Server Management Studio**.

Project 12.4	Using Distributed Queries
Overview	Queries are one of the most common activities in nearly any database application. In a distributed environment, they can include queries of the connected database server only and queries of remote data sources. Remote data sources can include additional instances of SQL Server and non–SQL Server data sources.
	One of the tools available for accessing a remote source, especially when retrieving data from a foreign source, is the use of rowset functions. One of the most commonly used of these is OPENROWSET, which retrieves data from a specified source and returns a rowset as its result. That rowset can then be used as a data source in a query or other operation. For security reasons, SQL Server 2005 disables ad hoc distributed queries by default. Before you can use OPENROWSET in an ad hoc query, you must enable ad hoc distributed queries.
	You also have the option of directly accessing the source in many situations. This requires that you fully qualify the source, including the server name, when working with a remote server. Access is usually through a pass-through query, a query sent to the remote server for execute. In SQL Server, you can use the OPENQUERY function to send pass-through queries.
Outcomes	After completing this project, you will know how to: ▲ use OPENROWSET to access remote data ▲ use OPENQUERY to retrieve data
What you'll need	To complete this project, you will need: ▲ a computer with two instances of SQL Server installed, each with its own version of the Chapter 12 sample database ▲ Microsoft Access and the Access sample files installed, to complete step 3 in the project
Completion time	45 minutes
Precautions	You must complete Project 12.3 before you can perform the steps in this project. In several commands, the command includes the replaceable text *computername*. In each instance, replace *computername* with your computer's name.

■ Part A: Prepare for queries and check the working environment

1. Launch **SQL Server Management Studio**. Connect to your default **SQL Server** instance.

2. Select **View** and then **Registered Servers**. How many registered servers are listed?

_____

_____

3. How any servers are listed in **Object Explorer**? Explain why.

_____

_____

4. Close the **Registered Servers** window.

■ Part B: Review OPENROWSET documentation

1. Select **Help** and then **Index.**
2. Type **OPENROWSET** in the **Look for:** field. In the topic list, select and review the **OPENROWSET** function and the **OPENROWSET** statement.
3. Close the **Help** window when finished reviewing.

■ Part C: Review and configure remote connection settings

1. Launch **SQL Server Surface Area Configuration**.
2. Click **Surface Area Configuration for Features**.
3. Select **Ad Hoc Remote Queries** under **Database Engine** and check **Enable OPENROWSET and OPENDATASOURCE support**.
4. Click **OK**, and then click **Surface Area Configuration for Service and Connections**.
5. Select **MSSQLSERVER**, then **Database Engine**, and then **Remote Connections**, as shown in Figure 12-5, and verify that the server is configured to support remote connections.

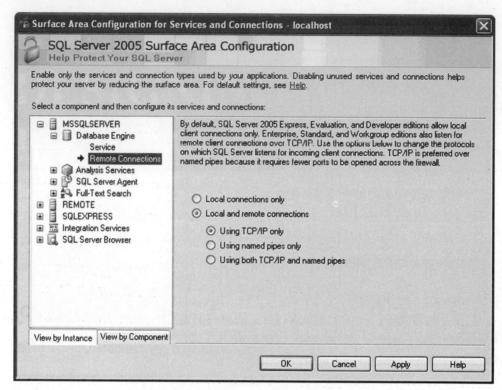

Figure 12-5: Remote connection support

6. Your server should be configured to support either TCP/IP only or TCP/IP and named pipes. It should NOT be configured for named pipes only.

7. Select **REMOTE**, then **Database Engine**, and then **Remote Connections**, and verify that the server is configured to support remote connections.

8. Click **OK**.

9. Exit **Surface Area Configuration**.

10. Shut down and restart your computer. Log in as an administrator when the computer restarts.

11. Launch **SQL Server Management Studio**.

12. Under your local server, expand **Databases**, right-click **Local12**, and select **New Query**. Verify that **Local12** is selected as the current database for the query window.

■ Part D: Use rowset functions

NOTE: Step 1 assumes that you have a **Microsoft Access** sample database installed in the default location. The path used is for **Office 2003, C:\Program Files\Microsoft Office\Office11\Samples**. Skip step 1 if you do not have Access installed.

1. Retrieve data from a foreign (not SQL Server) data source with OPENROWSET. In the query window, execute the following:

```
SELECT *
FROM OPENROWSET('Microsoft.Jet.OLEDB.4.0',
    'C:\ProgramFiles\MicrosoftOffice\OFFICE11\SAMPLES\Northwind.mdb';
    'admin';'', Customers)
```

2. If necessary, modify the path to the sample file if querying the sample from a different version of Microsoft Access. OPENROWSET connects to the file using the OLE_DB provider for the Microsoft Jet database engine, the sample Access file as the data source, 'admin' as the user name, a blank password, and the Customer table as the query. This returns all columns from the Customer table.

3. Execute the following to return the CustomerID and CompanyName columns only:

```
SELECT CustomerID, CompanyName
FROM OPENROWSET('Microsoft.Jet.OLEDB.4.0',
    'C:\ProgramFiles\MicrosoftOffice\OFFICE11\SAMPLES\Northwind.mdb';
    'admin';'', Customers)
```

4. How would you modify the query to filter the result horizontally?

_____

_____

_____

5. Retrieve data from a SQL Server database with OPENROWSET by executing the following in the query window:

```
SELECT a.*
FROM
OPENROWSET('SQLNCLI','Server=computername\REMOTE;Trusted_Connection=yes;',
    'SELECT *
    FROM Remote12.dbo.customer') a
```

NOTE: Replace *computername* with your computer's name. This is the server name for your default local SQL Server instance. For example, if your computer is named "DATADEV", you would run:

```
SELECT a.*
FROM
OPENROWSET('SQLNCLI','Server=machinename\REMOTE;Trusted_Connection=yes;',
    'SELECT *
    FROM Remote12.dbo.customer') a
```

6. Run a distributed join that retrieves SPNAME from the local SALESPERSON table and CUSTNAM out of the rowset returned by OPENROWSET, and joins the tables on SPNUM. OPENROWSET should return all rows and columns from the remote CUSTOMER table.

   a. What statement should you use?

       _____

       _____

   b. How could you reduce the traffic volume between the servers?

       _____

       _____

■ Part E: Use pass-through queries

1. Configure access to a remote server by creating a linked server. The linked server definition lets you specify security configuration information, including connectivity settings. Under your local server, expand server objects, then expand **Linked Servers**. What linked servers are currently listed?

       _____

       _____

2. Right-click **Linked Servers** and select **New Linked Server**.
3. Enter the server name as:

```
computername\REMOTE
```

Note: Replace *computername* with your computer's name.

4. Select **SQL Server**, as shown in Figure 12-6.

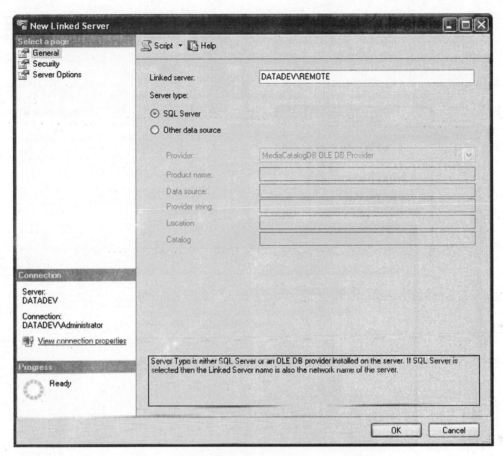

Figure 12-6: Linked server general options

5. Click **Security**. This lets you map logins from the local server to the remote server and set a default login context.

6. Select **Made using this security context**. Use **sa** as the login name and **P*55word** as the password. (**NOTE:** If you have changed the sa password on the remote server, use that password instead.) Why wouldn't you use this configuration in a production environment?

_____

_____

7. Click **OK**.

8. Use pass-through queries to access the server by, in the query window, executing the following:

```
SELECT * FROM
OPENQUERY([computermame\REMOTE],
'SELECT * FROM REMOTE12.DBO.CUSTOMER')
```

9. What does the query return?

   _____

   _____

10. Modify the query to return **CUSTNAME** and **CUSTNUM** only. What command would you use?

    _____

    _____

11. What would be the advantage of running the query this way?

    _____

    _____

12. Exit **SQL Server Management Server**. Do not save changes when prompted.

Project 12.5	Using Replication
Overview	Replication is used to keep remote databases consistent and up to date. You can use replication to create full or filtered copies of databases and keep the copies updated. Most DBMSs support a number of replication options, letting you create replication configurations to meet the requirements of nearly any situation you might encounter. SQL Server uses a publishing metaphor to describe replication. Replication databases are referred to as publications, with source tables referred to as article. Source computers are called publishers, and the computers that actually send the data are distributors. Destination computers are called subscribers, with subscriptions describing the information that they receive. SQL Server supports snapshot, merge, and transactional replication. Merge replication allows changes at the publisher or subscriber (source or destination) by default. Snapshot and transactional replication support changes at the publisher only by default, but both have configuration options to allow updating subscribers, that is, changes made at the subscriber.
Outcomes	After completing this project, you will know how to: ▲ enable replication ▲ configure a publication ▲ configure a subscription
What you'll need	To complete this project, you will need: ▲ a computer with two instances of SQL Server 2005 installed, each with its own version of the Chapter 12 sample database ▲ to have completed Project 12.3
Completion time	90 minutes
Precautions	This project requires a second, named SQL Server 2005 instance. To ensure that there are no problems with open transactions, unsaved configurations, and so forth, shut down and restart your computer before starting this exercise. If your computer has an instance of SQLEXPRESS installed, be careful that you do not use SQLEXPRESS as your remote server. The default settings will NOT match those provided in the activity steps if you use SQLEXPRESS. SQLEXPRESS will be present on the computer, for example, if you have installed Visual Studio on the computer.

■ Part A: Prepare for replication

1. Shut down and restart your computer. After the computer starts, log on as a local administrator. Launch **SQL Server Management Studio** and connect to your local server.
2. Open an **Object Explorer** connection to your "remote" server.

■ Part B: Create a transactional replication publication

1. Under your local server, expand **Replication**, right-click **Local Publications**, and select **New Publication**.
2. Click **Next** to continue past the **Welcome** screen. Leave the **Distributor** setting at its default (the local machine to act as its own distributor) and click **Next**.
3. Leave the snapshot folder at default and click **Next**.
4. When prompted with a list of publication databases, select **Local12** and click **Next**.
5. Select **Transactional publication** as the publication type and click **Next**. From the standpoint of updates, what is the significance of this choice?

   _____

   _____

6. Check , then expand **Tables**.

   a. Which tables will not be published?

   _____

   _____

   b. Why not? Click on the table if you need help.

   _____

   _____

7. Click **Article Properties** and choose **Set properties of all table articles**. Review the default property settings (DO NOT change the settings) and click **Cancel** to close the **Article Properties** dialog box when finished. The **Articles** settings should look like Figure 12-7. Click **Next** to continue.

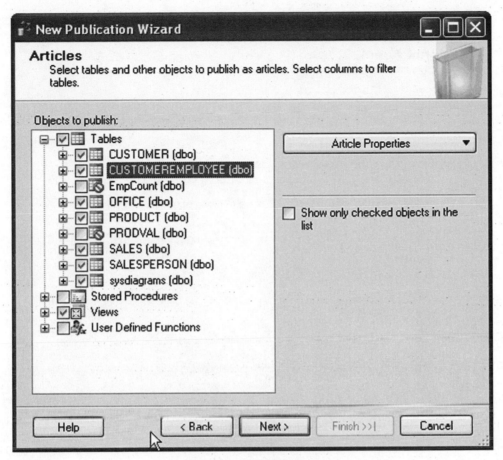

Figure 12-7: Articles settings

8. You do not want to configure any filtering at this time, so click **Next** to continue.
9. Choose to create the snapshot immediately, as shown in Figure 12-8, and click **Next** to continue.

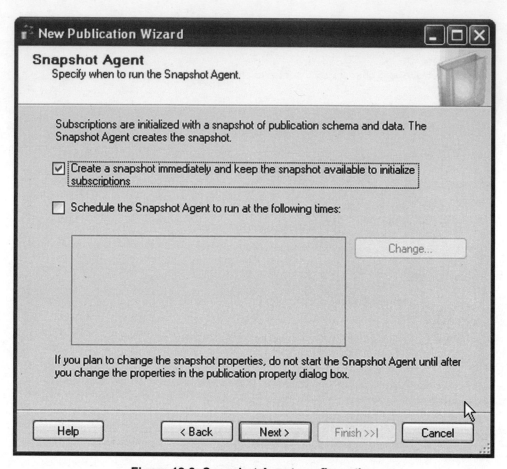

Figure 12-8: Snapshot Agent configuration

10. Click **Security Settings**, choose to run under the **SQL Server Agent** account (as shown in Figure 12-9), and then click **OK**. Should you use this as a production configuration?

_____

_____

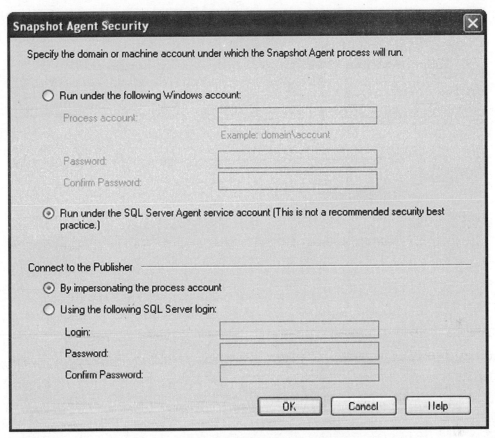

Figure 12-9: Snapshot Agent Security

11. Click **Next**.

12. Leave the wizard actions at default (**Create the publication**) and click **Next**.

13. Name the publication **AllLocal** and click **Finish**. A dialog box will inform you of progress.

14. Click **Close**.

15. Verify that the publication is listed under **Local Publications**.

■ Part C: Subscribe to the publication you just created from the "remote" server

1. Expand **Replication** under your remote server, right-click **Local Subscriptions**, and select **New Subscriptions**.

2. Click **Next** to continue past the **Welcome** screen.

3. In the **Publisher** drop-down list, select **<Find SQL Server publisher>** and connect to your local default instance. You should see the **AllLocal** publication listed as shown in Figure 12-10.

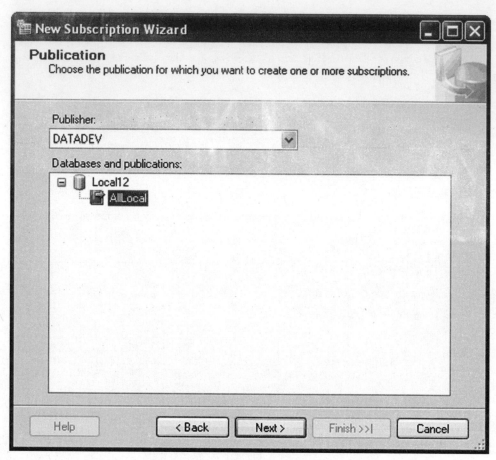

Figure 12-10: Available Publication

4. Verify that **AllLocal** is selected and click **Next**.

5. Leave the subscription type at default.

a. What is the default subscription type?

_____

_____

b. Which option places the least processing overhead on the distributor?

_____

_____

6. Click **Next** to continue.

7. Under **Subscription Database**, select **<New database>**. When prompted, name the database **Local12Copy**, set the file path for the database and log file to **C:\Chap12Remote**, leave the remaining settings at default, and click **OK**.

8. There will be a delay while the database is created. After the database is created, click **Next**.

9. Click the browse button **(…)** indicated in Figure 12-11.

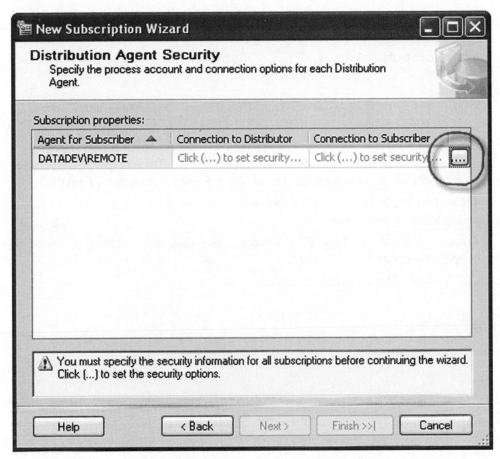

Figure 12-11: Security context browse button

10. Select to run under the SQL Server agent service account and click **OK**.

11. Click **Next**.

12. Set the synchronization agent schedule to **Run continuously** and click **Next**. What requirements does this place on the communication path between the servers?

_____

_____

13. Select to initialize the subscription immediately and click **Next**.

14. Leave the wizard actions at default and click **Next**.

15. Click **Finish** to create the subscription.

16. There will be a delay while the subscription is created. Click **Close** when finished.

17. Verify that the subscription is listed under **Local Subscriptions** for your remote server. Has the subscription list changed for the local server? Why or why not?

_____

_____

■ Part D: Verify that replication is working

1. Launch **My Computer** and navigate to **C:\Chap12Remote**. What files do you see listed?

    _____

    _____

2. Close **My Computer**.
3. In **SQL Server Management Studio**, under **Local Subscriptions** for your remote server, right-click the subscription and select **View Synchronization Status**.
4. Click **View Job History** and expand the first entry. This gives you an idea of the amount of activity generated by replication.
5. Click **Close** to close the **Log File Viewer**, and then click **Close** to close the **View Synchronization Status** dialog box.
6. Exit **SQL Server Management Studio**.

Project 12.6	Understanding Data Issues
Overview	Laws related to data and data security are changing constantly. This is especially true when accessing or transferring data across international boundaries. It is important to understand the laws that apply to your particular application and situation. In the United States, laws regarding data are set at both the state and the federal levels. Most countries have fewer laws related to data, but what they have usually covers similar issues, although they sometimes directly conflict with U.S. data requirements. In addition, there are guidelines specified by different standard organizations. Although these do not usually carry the weight of legal requirements, adherence is often necessary to facilitate communication between applications. Although it is possible to research data relations on the Internet, if you have significant international data requirements, you should consult with a legal expert.
Outcomes	After completing this project, you will know how to: ▲ discuss data regulatory requirements ▲ compare and contrast different countries' and standards organizations' requirements
What you'll need	To complete this project, you will need: ▲ a computer with Internet access
Completion time	60 minutes
Precautions	Any time you use Internet search engines, there is a possibility that you will be presented with links to inappropriate or offensive Web sites. Please review any information or summary provided by the search engine to try to determine if the link is appropriate. Some sites will attempt to install spyware or other malicious software when you connect. Review your security settings, and make sure that any security software installed on your computer is enabled and active before starting this activity.

Search for information related to data security regulations and restrictions on data access and data transfer. You should also look for sites that provide information about the potential legal ramifications of data ownership. Try various combinations of words in your search string to narrow your search.

1. What Web sites were you able to locate that provided appropriate information?

_____

_____

_____

_____

_____

_____

2. Which sites, if any, directly referred to laws and/or regulations that relate to international data transfers?

_____

_____

_____

_____

_____

_____

3. Based on your research, which country or region has the most restrictive laws and regulations regarding data security and transfer?

_____

_____

_____

_____

_____

_____

4. Which (if any stand out) have the least restrictive laws and regulations?

_____

_____

_____

_____

_____

_____

5. Provide specific examples of regulations or requirements and possible penalties for noncompliance.

_____

_____

_____

_____

_____

_____

6. What specifications did you find, if any, that define legal ownership of data?

_____

_____

_____

_____

_____

7. How do copyright regulations apply to data ownership issues?

_____

_____

_____

_____

_____

8. Are copyright laws consistent internationally? Explain your answer.

_____

_____

_____

_____

_____

_____

9. Why might concerns about data ownership impact a business? Give an example based on an actual business or business segment.

_____

_____

_____

_____

_____

_____